I0558631

Micro Conversations

The Hidden Power of Your Words on Mindset and Relationships

Dr. LaQuenta Long

Community Access

Unlock Exclusive Insights with the Weekly Wellness BOSS Newsletter!

Dear Reader, Thank you for diving into "Micro Conversations: The Hidden Power of Your Words on Mindset and Relationships." Your journey toward mastering effective communication and fostering meaningful relationships has just begun.

To continue receiving valuable insights, tips, and exclusive content on personal growth and wellness, I invite you to subscribe to the **Weekly Wellness BOSS Newsletter** by Dr. LaQuenta (also known as Dr. Quency).

What You'll Get:

- Expert Advice: Weekly tips on improving your

mindset, enhancing relationships, and boosting overall wellness.

- Exclusive Content: Access to articles, videos, and resources not available anywhere else.

- Community Support: Join a community of like-minded individuals committed to personal and professional growth.

- Special Offers: Be the first to know about upcoming events, new book releases, and special promotions.

How to subscribe:

1. Visit Dr. LaQuenta's Website.

2. Enter your email address in the subscription box.

3. Confirm your subscription via the email you receive.

4. Start your journey to a better you today! Don't

miss out on the valuable insights and support available though the Weekly Wellness BOSS Newsletter.

Warm regards,

Dr. LaQuenta

Click Stay Connected

Contents

About the Author   7

Introduction   9

Section 1: Understanding Micro Conversation   18

1. Everyday Words, Extraordinary Impact   19

2. Unpacking Communication   42

Section 2: Evaluating Your Micro Conversations   64

3. Understanding Your Inner Dialogue   65

4. Identifying Your Conversational Style   84

Section 3: Transforming Micro Conversations   95

5. Transforming Your Internal Dialogues   96

6. Self-Talk and Self-Perception: Why Your Words Matter   115

Section 4: Applying Micro Conversations in   131
Daily Life

7. Understanding Your External Conversations   132

8. Recognizing Barriers in Communication   146

9. Ensuring Long-Term Communication Suc-   161
    cess

Review   180

About the Author

Hello, I am LaQuenta Long, also known as Dr. Quency. I am a wife, mother, entrepreneur, licensed mental health therapist, crafter and so much more. As many of us play many roles in our day-to-day lives. I am also the founder of Design Life Hub, a community space dedicated to providing resources to support growth and care for mental health.

I have worked in the mental health industry for over 20 years. My educational background is a doctorate in clinical psychology, a masters in marriage and family therapy, applied behavioral analysis, and industrial/organizational psychology.

It is from both my personal and professional life experiences that I am excited to provide printed resources to support you in your personal growth, care, and accountability. Caring for your mental health doesn't have to start from addressing a problem. It's optimal when it becomes something we intentionally nurture every day through practice and skill development.

Introduction

Have you ever wondered how the smallest conversations can leave the biggest impact? Whether it's a brief chat with a stranger or a quick exchange with a friend, these micro conversations can shift the mood of your day. How different would your life be if you mastered the art of these seemingly insignificant exchanges?

That is the purpose of this book—to slow down and take an explorative look at the words you say to yourself as well as the conversations you share with others. There's a phrase many of us heard growing up: "Sticks and stones may break my bones, but words will never hurt me." As we both know, this isn't true. Words can hurt, and sometimes, the hurt they cause can take much longer to heal than physical injuries.

This book aims to uncover the hidden power of how we can use words to create change and support well-being beyond just positive affirmations. Positive affirmations set the stage for words to inspire us in a direction we desire. They are statements we make to ourselves to change perspective, but they are only one layer of harnessing the power of our words. These affirmations can also create conflict within because many times, the affirmations don't feel quite genuine. By learning to revise your micro conversations around a topic, you not only change the words you use but also influence the experience you have while saying them.

Micro conversations are about understanding how the words you say create the experiences you live in. Consider when you watch a movie—a captivating scene pulls you in and has you talking to the screen as if the actors can hear you. How does this happen? The writer of that scene has created a dialogue and image that engages you to respond.

The same thing happens when you read a book. For example, a romance novel with an exciting scene makes you feel what the character is feeling and leaves you curious about what will happen next. Just as the novel draws you into its world, your thoughts and the conversations you have with others can create similar experiences. They can change your mood, bring out emotions, and make you look forward to things.

What if you could become a better screenwriter for your own life, seeing how intentional words and created scenes in your conversations support the experiences you want to have?

How do you do this? That's the mindful review we're going to do with your micro conversations. We'll start by exploring what micro conversations are, in more detail. When you hear the word "conversations," it's understood that communication is happening as an exchange of ideas and information. We usually think of conversations between two or more people, but in this book will also talk about the inner thoughts you have as conversations to be mindful of.

We will learn about internal conversations by exploring what makes up a conversation. Be open to this learning journey. You will have "aha" moments when you realize things you didn't know you did in conversations. There will also be times for accountability where you think about things you already knew but sometimes forget. The goal of reviewing this information is to give you tools to take control of your conversations.

We will also review the style of communication and how we present information. The way we express ourselves to ourselves and others can determine whether or not someone will engage. Sometimes we get frustrated when, even though what we are saying makes sense, the other person isn't convinced. By exploring how we present our words and making necessary adjustments, you might be surprised at how much better your conversations can be.

The insights you gain throughout this book will help you change your conversations. Some talks are just for chatting, and that's okay. However, your intentionality becomes important when the conversations you're having no longer benefit you. It's about recognizing when discussions are unproductive and taking steps to break those unhealthy cycles. This will empower you to have more meaningful and supportive conversations that contribute to your overall well-being.

In my years of providing mental health services, I've seen repeatedly the power of conversation in a session. In our daily lives, we mostly share information and may expect some feedback, but we're not always mindful of how what we say elicits certain responses. Here, we're going to slow down and explore how you can take some of the conversational styles from a session into your everyday life.

I challenge you to read this book as a resource guide. It's informational in context, offering insights for you to consider. Reflect on what you read, relate it to yourself, and work on those parts. Some things may validate your feelings, while others might make you want to dismiss them. The goal is to reflect on the parts you can use to shift your conversations in a supportive way.

Give yourself the space to change the internal conversations you have that affect how you act and interact every day. Be intentional about the conversations you have with others. Know when to stop talking about a topic or change how you discuss it. Your conversations can support the experiences you have every day.

Expanding on Key Points

Power of Conversations

Conversations are not just exchanges of words; they are powerful tools that shape our reality. Every word we utter and every sentence we form can influence our mindset, emotions, and relationships. The key to harnessing this power lies in understanding the dynamics of our conversations and learning how to use them intentionally.

Internal and External Micro Conversations

Micro conversations can be both internal and external. Internal micro conversations are the thoughts and self-talk that occur within our minds. These internal dialogues can be positive or negative and can significantly influence our actions and perceptions. External micro conversations are the interactions we have with others. These small exchanges can have a lasting impact on our relationships and our emotional well-being.

Positive Affirmations

Positive affirmations are an important tool for shaping our self-talk. They help create a positive mindset and can motivate us to achieve our goals. But affirmations are just one part of using the power of our words. To truly benefit, we need to look deeper into how we use words in both our internal thoughts and conversations with others. Understanding your words not only reflects a thought, but creates an experience around what is said.

Becoming a Better Screenwriter

By being more thoughtful with our words, we can create the experiences we want. This means paying attention to how we talk to ourselves and others. Just like a screenwriter carefully designs a scene to get a certain reaction from the audience, we can shape our conversations to get positive responses and create supportive experiences.

Learning Journey

This book is a journey of self-discovery and growth. It will help you notice and understand the conversations you have with yourself and others. By recognizing patterns in these conversations, you can make changes to improve them. This way, you can take control of your words and use them to support your well-being and personal growth.

Practical Application

The insights and tools provided in this book are meant to be applied in your daily life. Whether it's changing how you talk to yourself or altering how you interact with others, these changes can lead to more positive and productive experiences. The goal is to help you become more intentional and mindful in your conversations, leading to a more fulfilling life.

The conversations we have with ourselves and others are important for shaping our lives. By understanding and using micro conversations, we can make positive changes, improve our relationships, and support our well-being. This book will guide you in mastering the art of conversations, helping you become more intentional and effective in how you communicate.

Section 1

Understanding
Micro Conversations

Chapter One

Everyday Words, Extraordinary Impact

O ur daily lives are full of constant communication. It's easy to miss the power of minor exchanges—those quick, seemingly unimportant talks we
have every day. Yet, these micro conversations can shape
our mindsets, influence our emotions, and change our
relationships. Whether it's the quiet self-talk that guides
our decisions or the brief chats with others that affect our
day, these subtle conversations hold great power. By un-

derstanding and mastering them, you can achieve personal growth and develop deeper connections.

Engaging in a conversation often feels second nature for those who find it easy to talk to anyone.

It's simply a matter of sharing your thoughts, experiences, and sometimes your opinions. This exchange flows naturally, as you smoothly move through topics and ideas, creating a natural rhythm of dialogue that feels both comfortable and engaging. You listen intently, responding with empathy and curiosity, allowing the other person or people to share their perspectives as well. This mutual exchange fosters a sense of connection and understanding, as both parties feel heard and valued. In this dynamic interplay, ideas are exchanged, relationships are strengthened, and just like that, a meaningful conversation has taken place, leaving everyone involved feeling enriched and understood.

And maybe this you can relate to.

Engaging in conversations can feel like navigating a maze for those who find them challenging.

A lot of preparation happens before they speak. This involves an internal dialogue where they anticipate how the other person might react to their words, weighing the potential outcomes of each remark. They might question whether to speak at all, and if they do, they carefully plan what to say next. This internal process can be exhausting. The focus shifts from choosing the right words to considering every nuance of the interaction. This includes the tone of voice, body language, facial expressions, and the overall context of the conversation. For them, conversations are complex puzzles where each piece must fit perfectly to avoid misunderstanding or discomfort. This heightened awareness and anxiety around every detail can make even casual interactions feel daunting, as they strive to navigate the intricacies of human communication with care and precision.

You might find yourself relating more to this example, or perhaps you fall somewhere in between. The key takeaway is that each of us has our own unique perspective on the ease of having a conversation.

In this book, I won't focus on every little detail in a conversation, but it's important to understand that what you say holds significance beyond the words themselves. The micro conversations you have with yourself, along with the simple interactions you share with others, can significantly impact your life experiences and relationships. Therefore, paying attention to these micro conversations is relevant. By being mindful of the messages you send to yourself and others, you can cultivate a more positive and constructive communication style.

What are micro conversations?

Conversations involve both a speaker and a responder in a two-way exchange, and in your internal micro conversations, you play both roles. These conversations go beyond self-talk; they reflect how your words influence you. When you think about something your body responds. This might be change in your body language where maybe you cross your arms. It could be an internal shift where your heart begins to race. And some times it simply the comment you say internally to the first thought you had.

We engage in micro conversations all day long, not just with others, but also with ourselves. During daily routines like making coffee or driving to work, you might review your to-do list, plan dinner, or reflect on your day. These brief moments help you process experiences, plan, and prepare for what's next, shaping your mood and mindset.

Sometimes, these internal dialogues occur before speaking to someone. In a meeting, for example, you might weigh the pros and cons of a colleague's suggestion before responding. With your child, if they ask to stay up past their bedtime, you think about their recent sleep patterns, the impact of your response, and the principles you want to teach. Your reply is shaped by this micro conversation.

As an athlete, I used to coach myself during runs, focusing on one mile at a time and giving myself mini pep talks. These small messages helped me get through my race. Think about the little things you say to yourself. These words set the tone for what you do next.

Micro conversations also occur when talking to others. Two types exist: internal conversation before speaking and small, frequent exchanges during the day.

Internal conversations while talking with someone else:

Internal conversations can significantly impact your interactions. Sometimes, you may respond more to your internal dialogue than to the actual words spoken by others. Your internal conversation is reflective of your interpretation of the conversation. You may edit the actual words of the other person by adding your perspective. This can often times influence the way you respond back in the conversation.

Micro conversations that are had frequently with others:

Repeated small exchanges, such as saying, "They're always late" or "She never listens", might seem minor but can become significant over time. These small comments create a perception of a person or a situation. Micro conversation that are repeated on a topic after multiple discussion can develop a default scenario that you refer back to without always considering present day circumstances.

Recognizing and understanding these micro conversations can enhance your self-awareness and improve your interactions with others.

Why do your micro conversations matter?

Micro conversations are the small, often fleeting interactions we have with ourselves and others. Even though these conversations are short, they have a big impact on how we think, feel, and act. Understanding why micro conversations matter can help us see their effects and use this insight to make changes in future conversations.

Here's something you might not always realize about the conversations you have with yourself and others: you are creating experiences. These experiences reveal whether someone is interested in you, and whether they show support, care, or love.

Conversations shape how we perceive others and how they perceive us. They reveal if someone values your input and validates your perspective. They can also show alignment with your point of view. The context of a conversation goes beyond the words spoken and holds significant importance.

This book will discuss how to maximize conversations, filter out key takeaways, and end unhelpful ones.

The time you give to micro conversations.

The thing you talk about the most, you hear the most as well. It is a constant message that is given on repeat. The time given to discussing carves out a place in your everyday existence. Before you know it, it forms your dominate point of view on a topic.

When you spend more time talking about something, maintaining that point of view becomes easier. You can go on autopilot with your thoughts, feelings, and expressions. The people in your life can predict what you will say about certain things. Sometimes, your conversations become something where you really don't think about what you are saying.

Think about this for a moment. Have you ever walked into work and said. "Ugh, is it Friday yet?" Now, consider how many days start off like that. At the moment you said it, did anything specific happen that influenced why you felt that way?

This example reflects how habitual conversations can shape our daily mindset without any specific trigger. These automatic responses become ingrained in our routine, affecting our mood and outlook. Recognizing these patterns is essential because they show how our thoughts and words influence our overall well-being.

Evaluating the Impact of Micro Conversations

The micro conversations you have reflect the importance you place on the topic at hand. It doesn't necessarily mean it's something you deeply cherish. The time given to certain micro conversations often reflects their hierarchy of relevance in your life.

For example, if you spend a lot of time discussing work related topics, it likely means that work issues are highly relevant to you at the moment. On the other hand, if you rarely talk about your hobbies, it might indicate that they are currently less significant in your daily life.

Understanding this hierarchy helps you recognize which areas are consuming your attention and may need to be balanced or adjusted based on your priorities and goals.

We should reflect on the importance of both significance and time given to our conversations. The significance of certain topics in your life can be prioritized, especially when it comes to key areas like parenting or your marriage. You can connect important parts of your life to what you are striving to overcome or achieve.

Emphasizing significance in your talks can highlight what is most important to you. By sharing your values and priorities, you help others understand what drives you. By showcasing what matters to you, deeper connections can be created.

Gaining knowledge through conversations is another key aspect. Whether learning from others' experiences or discussing new ideas, these interactions contribute to your personal growth. Some conversations might be quick and to the point, offering nuggets of wisdom. Others might be more extensive, allowing for in-depth exploration of a topic. The reason conversations occur is their significance. They are not just about exchanging words, but about creating meaningful interactions. These discussions enrich your personal connections and enhance your understanding.

Sometimes you talk about politics, work, or other people's lives even if they don't affect you directly. Conversations like these gain value from time invested, not significance. You have intentionally or unintentionally carved out a space in your life. Think about it. Do you spend more time on sports than talking about your kids? Do you spend more time discussing office shenanigans than what is happening in the people's lives you live with? The significance of these things you may discuss is not greater than the comparison. They hold value in your life because of the significant talk time given to them.

The picture you paint for yourself

The micro conversations you have create a layered picture of whatever you are discussing. Let's consider a positive scenario. These micro conversations might focus on your determination. Internal statements like "You got this," "Just a few more things to do and you'll be done," or "It's worth it; keep going" help build your vision. As you say these things, you start to see what it will take to achieve your goal. You are constructing a mental image of success and predicting the next steps. Micro conversations are like small brush strokes on a canvas. Each one adds detail to an image that will eventually become a complete picture. This picture then serves as a reference for future reflections.

The picture you create for yourself comes from both your internal conversations and the ones you have with others. For example, consider the conversations you have with your supervisor about work tasks. You might submit a task for review and receive feedback that either requires correction or grants approval. In that moment, you might feel a sense of accomplishment or inadequacy. Similarly, an email from your supervisor listing additional responsibilities can either be seen as a sign of trust and increased responsibility, or just another item on your to-do list. Each of these interactions is a micro conversation.

Remember, conversations occur both within yourself and with others, and your responses—whether spoken or unspoken—help paint each stroke of the overall picture being formed.

The picture you paint for others

It's one thing to face the picture you paint for yourself; it's another thing entirely to face the picture you paint for others. Before I talk about the way micro conversations influence these images, I am going to encourage you not to go to a place of judgment. The purpose of learning is not to harm yourself with the information you gain. It is a resource you use to grow and change. In later chapters, I will discuss ways to make changes and introduce small shifts in how you interpret these conversations. For now, the focus is on awareness.

Let's look at some examples of how this happens. In a conversation, you share information about a topic, express your feelings, or outline steps you plan to take. Each conversation adds strokes to the canvas of your image. For instance, if you're discussing your job and say things like,

"I never have time to breathe," "I can't seem to catch up," or "Today, I did ten things but still didn't make a dent in my work," these statements paint a picture of being overwhelmed, constantly busy, or lacking enough time. Even if you love your job, these comments create an image of frustration and dissatisfaction.

If most of your conversations focus on negative aspects, others will see a negative picture of your work experience. They won't know about the positive aspects unless you also talk about what you enjoy and appreciate.

Another example is when you seek help from others about someone or something. These conversations can be tricky because they often highlight negative points. For now, we're focusing on awareness. Later, I'll discuss how to handle these conversations productively, including choosing the right person to talk to and setting the stage for effective communication.

When talking to others about your child, you might say things like, "My child keeps making wrong decisions," "Will this kid ever learn?" or "I don't think my kid even listens to me." These statements paint a picture of your child's behavior and your frustration. It's important to realize that these conversations shape how others view your situation. You can intentionally paint a more balanced picture by also sharing positive reflections and your hopes for improvement.

Future influencers

The simplicity of a small conversation can take on a lingering effect. It reminds me of our social media feeds. Every so often, you come across a post from one year ago. When you initially posted, you weren't thinking about how it will feel when this comes up on your feed a year from now. You're probably not thinking about how different your life might be when that post shows up in your feed again in the future. The only thing you are considering at the moment of your post is what is going on in that moment.

Similar to our social media post, our micro conversations can resurface in a layering effect. A sort of building blocks of evidence that can be supportive or destructive in their future use. Consistent conversations can have a greater impact over time, even if they may seem insignificant initially. A simple comment about how you look in an outfit can carry over into other moments when you have similar thoughts.

Understanding the future effects of micro conversations is not about being over critical of everything you say. It is giving considerations to those moments when you have a bigger reaction to a simple statement. It is in the awareness of how the things you say now can resurface in a way unattended. To create relevant filters for the conversations you have had and with whom you have them with.

The undertone of future conversations

Have you ever been to a restaurant and ordered some fries that had a little different flavor from what you were expecting? Like something else was fried in the oil other than fries. The flavor of the previous fried food has now influenced the taste of your fries. This is how simple conversations of the past can sometimes influence future conversations.

Think about it. You have a problem with someone you are dating, and you talk about it with your best friend. The problem eventually gets resolved, but the conversation you had about it remains part of future discussions with that friend. Or maybe you made a mistake once on a project at work. You comment within yourself about what you did wrong and how you feel about yourself because of the mistake. Then later, when asked to take part in another project, you almost immediately consider the potential things that could go wrong.

Being aware of your conversations allows you to understand what affects your reactions in different situations. It supports learning whom to have conversations with. Recognizing and addressing the undertones in your conversations involves being aware that they exist in the first place. Being in tune with these subtle cues helps you shift the direction and tone of your interactions.

Reference tool in future conversations

Micro conversations often influence the future by becoming reference points that people use for or against you.

And this includes you too. Think about when you were going through school, and you had to write a paper. There were certain occasions that your assignment required you to cite other documents that supported your point of view on the topic of discussion. Your teacher most likely gave you some guidelines on the type of material that could be cited. This was in place to ensure the credibility of your cited source.

Your past conversations become the cited source of future conversations. Comments like "Remember when you said" or "You always say"; it might be even "You told me that." However phrased, the things you say in simple conversation become a reference tool to confirm the relevance of what you are saying at this moment. The micro conversation can be a point of accountability for the choices you make. It can serve as a standard by which you are held accountable. These conversations can acts as a reminder of your previous stance. Or it is used as a measure of consistency based on past conversations. Being mindful of what you are talking about and how often you are talking about it has significance. When you account for your conversations beyond the moment, you challenge yourself to consider how it shows up later.

Influences on future decisions

Why do athletic coaches do a pep talk before a game begins? What is the purpose of time-outs once a game is in motion? What is the value in having half-time huddles? It is in these brief conversations that the coach's goal is to reset the team's outlook on the game. It is to provide guidance and accountability. To shift the players' focus on their individual actions and how they can influence the overall game's outcome. A small conversation in that moment can literally be the game-changing conversation for the outcome of the game.

The same is true for the micro conversations you take part in. They send brief messages about your situation, your abilities, perspective, and more. In these simple conversations, you gather the information needed to form your next steps. Whether you have future experiences in a relationship, whether you talk to your boss about your work experiences, it can influence whom you trust in a relationship.

These small conversations can have an impact bigger than the moment in which you first have them. A coach understands if I can challenge this player to use the information, I present over what the player is experiencing, I can guide them to the outcome desired. Coaches help players look beyond their immediate circumstances by requiring them to draw on resources and focus on what has been said. The power of those words influences the decisions they will make when the game resumes. Recognize the power that a micro conversation can have when you are aware of its potential impact.

Used as a filter for the future

The influence of your micro conversations as a resource can be significant as you continue to gain awareness. Have you ever used affirmations in your daily routine? These power statements affirm beliefs about yourself and beliefs about your future. The benefits of affirmations are to center your thinking positively. The hope is to focus on the good traits that support the outcome of what you desire. It is to incorporate these affirmations into your daily, weekly, and monthly routines. It extends the influence of your affirmations in how you experience people and the world around you. This is where micro conversations come into play.

Affirmation is one part of micro conversations. Remembering micro conversation is the combination of what is said and how one responds to it. Recognizing responses are not just the audible words you speak. Micro conversations also have a layering aspect to them. If you only say affirmations once a day, then the other conversations you have throughout the day will dominate and shape how you interpret your experiences.

Consider for a moment whether you are asked to speak at an event. In your past, you had a terrible experience where you didn't do well. You have affirmed you will do well and that you can get up and speak at this upcoming event. The filter of your micro conversations comes into play when you talk to the surrounding people. Are you maintaining your affirmations or are you talking about your relevant fears? Are they talking back to you in ways to align with your affirmations, or are they reflecting on what went wrong the last time?

Micro conversations can act as a filter to future situations and how you see your abilities in those situations. How you talk about the things you remember shapes a picture. It is in those images you consider the likely outcome of future events. This happens with the good and the bad. The goal is to understand that your micro conversations play a role in how you filter what comes next. It influences how you determine what you will use in future events.

Your conversations matter

Taking the time to learn about micro conversations is about creating a resource in the words you speak. The ones that happen with others and the ones you are having with yourself. It is not for you to be overly cautious about everything you say. There is a time and a place to fine-tune the details of what you communicate. The information

I will share, use as a tool to help change your conversations when needed. You will work to understand when change is not happening in a sustained manner to consider the conversations you are having around it. To place your conversations in a place to be a resource and minimize its effects as a roadblock.

Chapter Two

Unpacking Communication

B asic rules exist for good conversations. Knowing these rules can help you talk to people better. Every part of a conversation gives you a chance to influence change with your words. By paying attention to how you speak, you can change how your conversations turn out.

When we look at micro conversations, we'll talk about things like the topic, your opinions, and your feelings about it. These things influence your self-talk and communication with others. Understanding what makes up your micro conversations is part of how you work to change them on purpose. In this chapter, we'll go over different parts of this. Not all of them might fit you, but they should help you understand how to break down and think about your own conversations.

Topic of Discussion

The topic is the first consideration in a conversation. This is what you are talking about, like family, school, politics, or friends. It's the main idea you are focusing on. There are three ways to discuss a topic: focusing on the present, considering the future, and reflecting on the past. This means that the information you share is related to a specific time.

In present-day focus, the conversation is on what is happening now. It's all connected to the present. For example, when you come home and talk about work, you might share your current stress: "My boss told me to fix the documents I submitted," or "I got two more projects to handle." You're only talking about the things affecting your stress today.

Another example is talking about relationships. Regardless of past issues, a present-day conversation solely addresses recent effects of one's actions on the other. You might say, "When you didn't come home on time, I was worried," or "When you didn't call me back, I thought you were mad." The focus is on recent events.

In contrast, a past-focused conversation references historical triggers. For instance, with work stress, you might say, "My boss is always correcting my work," or "Each time I think I'm wrapping up a project, I get more projects to oversee." The topic is still work stress, but the focus is on past events rather than current ones.

In relationships, past-focused comments might be, "You keep coming home late, and I can't depend on you," or "Our whole marriage, you've put off calling me back when you say you will." Here, the emphasis is on the history of the experience, not just the recent incident.

The last focus is future-focused. This perspective projects what will happen in the future. The main theme remains the same, but the information connects to future expectations. For example, you might say, "I don't think my boss will ever stop giving me corrections," or "The projects on my to-do list will keep piling up." The topic is work stress, but the outlook is on what's coming.

In relationships, future-focused comments might be, "You will always come home late," or "I doubt you will ever call me back when you say you will."

The main idea of a conversation sets the tone and direction of the discussion. The tone changes depending on whether you focus on the present, past, or future. For example, if you're talking about work stress, the tone might be about handling current tasks (present), dealing with past issues (past), or thinking about what to expect (future). The way you speak sets the tone for the conversation and can influence how you or others respond. This can help in finding solutions and figuring out what to do next.

Behind the scenes: personal thoughts and opinions

Even if you don't say some things out loud, they still show in how you act and speak. These unspoken words reveal your opinions, experiences, and attitude about the topic. Sometimes, what you say doesn't match what you feel. This happens because you're trying to be nice or fit the situation, but your genuine message can get lost.

Even if you don't speak, your message can come through in other ways, like your body language, tone of voice, and choice of words. For example, crossing your arms, avoiding eye contact, or having a tense posture can show you're uncomfortable or disagreeing, even if your words are polite. A sarcastic or flat tone can show you don't mean what you're saying. Speaking too softly might make you seem unsure, while a loud voice can show you're frustrated or angry.

This mismatch between what you say and what you mean can cause misunderstandings. For example, if you say, "I'm fine," but look upset, the other person might get confused or doubt you.

It's important to understand the micro conversations you have with yourself. These inner thoughts affect how you talk to others. Knowing your own thoughts and feelings helps you make sure your words and actions match. This makes your communication clearer and more honest.

Knowing your own inner conversations helps you see when you're not being clear. By noticing this, you can work on expressing yourself more honestly, making sure your messages are clear and consistent.

Your opinion on the subject

Sometimes, to get along with others, you might not share your full opinion. You might say you love something just to make someone feel good, even if you don't. You can keep talking to a co-worker even if they annoy you. Your personal thoughts might not always add to the conversation.

Understanding the parts of your conversation and knowing your perspective is important for choosing your tone and words. Let's talk about tone. The tone of your conversation shows how you feel about the topic. If you have a negative outlook, your comments might be dismissive or argumentative. But if you have a positive outlook, you are more likely to be curious and engaged. Your inner thoughts often come out unfiltered. If you've learned tools for self-talk or self-regulation, your micro conversations help manage your initial thoughts. This internal conversation influences what you say out loud.

When choosing the words to speak out loud, acknowledging the sensitivity of the topic may lead you to be more selective in your phrasing. Your words might be fewer or more measured to address the awkwardness of the conversation. They may be more sensitive and less focused on addressing the issue at hand. Internal micro conversations give space for your personal opinions, but it's important not to disregard how they can still manifest in your audible conversation.

Your past associations with the topic of discussion

The past is a powerful resource. It can support the outcome you desire, delay it, or even destroy it. This might sound dramatic, but it's true. Think about it. Have you ever felt accomplished by something? Have you ever received a compliment? Someone might say, "You look nice today," "That was a great presentation; I learned a lot," or "You have a great kid." Whatever the compliment, it shifts your experience at that moment. You walk a little differently, feel more joyful, and your outlook changes.

Now, fast-forward in time. You're in your closet and come across the outfit you were complimented on. A smile comes to your face. You remember the compliment and decide to wear that outfit again.

Or maybe you're asked to speak at a bigger meeting than ever before. You think about the good feedback from your past presentations and realize you can do this one. So, you say yes to the invitation.

Your experiences become little reminders of what was.

Sadly, unpleasant experiences are harder to turn into something good. Maybe you've been in a relationship where someone kept pointing out your flaws. Or maybe you've had a boss who criticized even the smallest things you did. These moments replay in your mind, stopping you from trying new things or keeping you in unhealthy relationships.

Remember, the past can be a powerful resource, even the moments that hurt or disappoint you. The key is how you think about these experiences. The micro conversations you have moving forward are shaped by these past moments, depending on what you choose to focus on.

Instead of dwelling on negative comments, your micro conversation can acknowledge that the relationship was unhealthy. You focus on what you want in the future and how you can improve yourself. You also recognize the importance of being with someone who supports you.

Your micro conversations decide what your experiences mean to you in the future. They affect both current and future talks about those topics. When a friend asks for relationship advice or when your boss gives you a task, these micro conversations guide your responses. Even if you don't say them out loud, they influence what you say.

Your emotional connection

Your emotions matter. There are emotional experiences you would prefer to avoid because they are uncomfortable. If you had it your way, you would cut them out of your life. But I say to you, if those emotions were absent, you would be missing a significant tool for navigating life.

Your emotional connection to a topic being discussed can highlight its value to you. If it is something you love, your ability to advocate for it or your desire to protect it comes out in your conversation. If it is something that causes hurt, your focus might be to object to the idea or avoid talking about it altogether.

Emotions are not always described in conversation, but they can shift the intensity of the dialogue.

Consider a conversation with your child where you are trying to get them to focus more on their schoolwork. You give them tips on how to study, but instead of responding to your help, they withdraw, give you attitude, or are dismissive. In that moment, you might maintain an even tone and say encouraging words, but your child's micro conversation is connected to feelings of disappointment, hurt, sadness, or regret. These emotional connections can outweigh the actual words being said.

Micro conversations are the talks you have with yourself and others. Conversations filled with strong emotions leave a bigger impact than those with less feeling. These private thoughts influence how you behave in a conversation. To be more thoughtful in your conversations, it's important to understand this.

How you present information

You have a usual way of sharing information in a conversation—your default style. This default style shows how you understand and process information. Basically, you talk in the way you like to hear information.

For example, some people talk in a direct and clear way, getting straight to the point. This shows they value being clear and efficient when sharing and receiving information. They probably like it when others talk to them in the same straightforward way.

Some people like to give lots of details and background information when they talk. This shows they value a deep understanding and like to see the complete picture. They enjoy conversations that explore topics in depth and appreciate when others take the time to explain things thoroughly.

The way you present information can also show how you think and feel. For example, if you talk with lots of energy and excitement, it might show that you are passionate about the topic and want to connect with others emotionally. If you speak in a calm and careful way, it might show that you prefer to think things through and focus on facts rather than feelings.

Understanding your usual way of talking is important because it affects how others see you and how well you can share your message. It also helps you understand why some ways of talking feel right to you while others seem hard or uncomfortable.

By knowing your natural way of talking, you can change your style to fit different situations and people better. For example, at work, you might need to use a more formal tone, while with friends, a relaxed style might be more appropriate.

Ultimately, recognizing and understanding your default communication style enhances your ability to connect with others, facilitates clearer and more effective interactions, and allows you to tailor your approach to achieve the desired outcomes in various conversational contexts.

Detailed play-by-play of the event

The message is in the details. In communication, you might be the person who values providing each detail associated with the discussion. It's not about showing how smart you are; the details just matter. When details are crucial in conversations, it involves thoroughly covering the topic, including the information you've gathered from various sources, your thoughts on the matter, and the context behind your opinions. It's not enough to simply share your personal thoughts; you must also explain what led you to feel that way. Your micro conversations are layered with a lot of information.

However, there is a balance to be struck. Presenting too many insignificant details may cause your audience to lose interest or miss the main point. Overloading a conversation with details can dilute the impact of your message, making it harder for listeners to grasp the essential points.

If this internal micro conversation is filled with too many details, it can make it hard for you to make decisions. When your mind is stuck on details, you might find it hard to figure out what to do next. This can lead to "analysis paralysis," where you're so focused on details that you can't take the next steps.

Evaluating the need for change is essential for tailoring micro conversations when details matter. This involves being mindful of your audience and the context of the conversation. Ask yourself: What are the key points that need to be communicated? Which details are necessary to support these points? What information can be omitted without losing the essence of the message?

For example, in a work presentation, instead of going into every minor detail, focus on the most important facts that support your point. Give enough detail to be clear, but not so much that it gets confusing. In personal conversations, pay attention to the listener. If they seem bored, it might be a sign to shorten your message.

While details can make a conversation better, they should be used carefully. Good communication means balancing detailed information with being clear and brief. By knowing how much detail is right for the situation, you can make sure your message both informative and interesting.

Your interpretation only of the events

Another way to share information is by focusing only on your point of view. You talk about how it made you feel, your view of events, and your thoughts on the topic. In these conversations, it's clear what you think. The challenge is being open to others' views. You might focus so much on your thoughts that you see them as facts, instead of just your experience.

This way of talking can make your view seem more important than what actually happened. For example, if you talk about a fight with a classmate, you might focus on how unfairly you were treated without thinking about the bigger picture or their side. This can create a biased story that changes how you remember and understand the experience.

Changing micro conversations means focusing on what really happened, not just what you think happened. It means recognizing the facts and being open to other viewpoints. For example, instead of saying, "I was treated unfairly," you could describe what was said and done and then talk about how it made you feel. This way, you separate the events from your feelings, allowing for a more balanced view.

It's important not to stick only to your version of events. Listen actively and try to understand others' viewpoints to gain a fuller picture of the situation. Hearing what others have to say adds valuable context to your own experiences and feelings. This broader perspective helps you see things more clearly, improving communication and relationships.

While it's natural to focus on your own point of view, it's important to balance it with being open to others' perspectives. Doing this can help you grow and improve your interactions. This means not only changing how you think about your experiences, but also being willing to listen and learn from new information and ideas.

Projection of what is going to come based on interpretation

Sometimes, talking about something means describing how it might affect the future. In these cases, you focus on what you think will happen next because of the topic. You're more concerned with how you'll deal with it in the future, not just what's happening right now.

These conversations might go like, "My boss said we are having a meeting tomorrow. We'll probably get told off for messing up the project." You're already deciding how the meeting will go before it happens. This can affect how you feel and lead to more inner talks during the meeting.

When you talk about what might happen, it can be both good and bad. On the positive side, it helps you get ready mentally and emotionally for what could come. This way, you can plan your actions and responses better, which might lead to better results.

However, this way of thinking can also have downsides. If you think too negatively, it can cause stress and worry. For example, expecting the worst about the upcoming meeting might make you feel nervous or defensive, which can hurt your performance and interactions. This negative attitude can affect not only how you feel but also how others react to you.

The key to talking about the future is managing the picture you create. This means balancing realistic expectations with a positive outlook. Instead of just focusing on what might go wrong, think about the good things, too. For example, you could say, "My boss scheduled a meeting tomorrow. It's a chance to talk about the project and learn how we can do better next time."

Doing this sets a more positive tone for your thoughts about the meeting. This balanced approach helps you stay open to feedback and more involved in finding solutions. It can improve your attitude, making you more resilient and able to handle different situations.

While it's important to get ready for future events, it's also crucial to manage how you think about them. Focus on a balanced view, not just your own opinions. This helps you handle conversations and situations better, leading to more positive results.

Who you talk to matters

In a conversation, who you're talking to can affect your word choice, openness, and intensity. Who you talk to can influence the direction you go in a conversation. The person you talk to matters.

Consider it for a moment. Think about conversations with a parent. Are there things you might add or take away when talking about your spouse? Are there areas you emphasize about a situation? Is there a way you talk with your best friend that might look different from how you talk with co-workers? The topic of discussion stays the same, but what and how you say it shifts.

How is this relevant to your micro conversations? It is relevant in two ways: the words spoken and the frequency you hear them.

Remember, your micro conversations significantly affect how you experience the topic of discussion.

The words you choose in a conversation can either reveal or conceal parts of yourself that you want others to know. Your focus might be on parts of a situation that would influence them to agree with your perspective. It might also be words you use to downplay your part.

Your words influence both you and the person you are speaking to. For yourself, you are reinforcing the image you have created about the topic. For the other person, they are forming their own perspective based on what you have said. In shaping the conversation this way, you have limited their responses by framing the topic in a specific way.

Sometimes, the selection of whom you talk to is influenced by how you can manage the feedback they give you.

Your micro conversations are important in shaping the bigger picture, so you need to pay attention to what you say and how often you talk about it. If you only talk to certain people, you'll only hear one version of the conversation. This can be both helpful and harmful, depending on the situation.

Say, for instance, you are looking to make some changes in your life. You decide to only express your thoughts to people who are supportive of the changes you want to make. You openly discuss your efforts, downfalls, and approaches. These conversations are the input you are frequently exposed to. After a while, there comes a consistency and flow to them. This can be helpful when you previously desired to change but were met with diverse input on what and how you should do it. However, limiting your conversation may not be your first step to getting to this place.

The harm in only having a small selection of people to talk to is filtering whether you are on the right path in shaping your conversations. A little healthy opposition can be resourceful. It's important to know when to narrow the group to a few. Maybe you need to be challenged if your focus is not getting you the results that will be helpful for you. The awareness comes in who those people will be and when to narrow it only to that group.

When considering whether the people you are having micro conversations with are appropriate, there are some things to consider in your selection. Think about why you have chosen them to talk about the topic, as well as why you might avoid them. Also, consider the ways you filter your conversation on the topic with certain people.

How you talk in a conversation is intentional, even if you don't realize it. The key is to become more aware. This makes your micro conversations more useful. It helps you control their impact. Micro conversations let you take charge of what influences your daily life.

Section 2

Evaluating Your
Micro Conversations

Chapter Three

Understanding Your Inner Dialogue

Micro conversations, which are the continuous internal dialogues we have, are influenced by various factors. In this chapter, we will explore the different influencers that shape these micro conversations. These include how you perceive yourself, the interpretations you have of others, your past experiences, and your levels of inspiration. Your self-perception forms the basis of how you talk to yourself, while your understanding of other people's views provides an additional layer to what becomes your internal dialogue. Past experiences serve as reference points, shaping how you react and make decisions. Meanwhile, your inspiration levels determine the tone and direction of your thoughts, whether positive or negative. By understanding these influencers, you can gain better control over your micro conversations and use them to your advantage.

Your version of you

You already have a sound idea of who you are, shaped by your experiences and how you interpret them. At any moment, something can remind you of a past event. Instead of focusing only on the present and the conversation happening with others, you might also think about these past experiences. This creates an internal dialogue that only you are aware of, while having an external conversation with someone else.

There are three main types of reflections you might have in different situations. These can focus on past hurts or disappointments, past experiences with your abilities, and "what if" thoughts about the future. These reflections help you understand yourself and shape how you react in different situations.

Let's start with things from your past. One unpleasant experience can dominate the conversational tone once it has happened. Think of an occasion where you had to search for a job. Consider what it was like to interview for the jobs you had applied for. Think of those moments where the interview did not go so well. Now fast forward in time to a job search experience that followed that one. How much did your conversation, as you prepared for the interviews in this cycle, take into account what happened before? How many times did your opinion about how you would perform was based on the last round of interviews? Or maybe your conversation was about coaching yourself on what you should do differently because of what happened the last time.

Past disappointments can be the center of many conversations, even when the event itself happened a long time ago. The extent of your past is kept relevant in the micro conversations that you have with yourself. Your reflection on your ability to do something can stem from past experiences, but it also becomes something you continuously create and shape beyond any single event. Sometimes you can define your ability to do something and not be able to give a reason you think that way.

This can show up in your micro conversations sounding like "I can't speak in front of others," or "I am not the person who can . . .," or possibly "I wish I could, but it is just not me." When asked why you say this, your answer is vague or dismissive. You have pre-defined your abilities for the future based on the past. Sometimes the statements you make are accurate. While other times, they're based on an interpretation of what you believe to be true. No matter how you arrived at your decisions, your abilities are shaped by your micro conversations. These internal dialogues influence your actions and decisions in the moment.

What-ifs can be another common conversation that you are having with yourself. You reflect on the future possibilities of people in your life. The internal conversations suggest a direction you should take regarding an upcoming event. These micro conversations can become a centering truth you decide from. You have discussed them within yourself so often that maybe you remove all questions of them being a what-if. The shift becomes more focused on "what will be."

This frame of conversation can serve you in a way that supports the future you desire. And at times, it can work against you. When you can align what-if conversations with the outcome desired, it can be a resource to keep you accountable for your future.

Learning to have a what-if conversation helps you set the tone by saying, "In this relationship, I will establish trust. I can learn to hear what my partners says and accept it as the truth. I won't get wrapped in my opinions, but honor the things that are happening for what they are." These what-if conversations support the way you want to show up in a relationship. It is an encouraging step you will take towards trust. It becomes a coaching conversation about what to expect of yourself.

To shape conversations like this, you need to have a clear goal in mind and use words that align with it.

Interpretation of how others think about you

The internal conversations you have about how others see you play a big role in how you act and present yourself. These thoughts about what others might say, think, or do can be influential. Sometimes, your self-perception clashes with how you believe others see you. This can be confusing and complicated, making it even harder to process.

The conversations you are having with yourself about what someone considers you to be can shape decisions. You say to yourself, "I am not capable of ___ because he thinks I am not a leader." Or, "Everyone knows I am not the person you go to for ___." Or maybe, "I can see in the way they look at me, that they think I am ___." You interpret the cues you read from someone's body language as their opinion of you. There might have been that one time someone said something to you, that you have made their ongoing perspective of you. Or it could be that interpretation of you is what you have been in the past, but it's not the you that you are now. The version of what they think, believe, consider is kept alive with the conversations you have with yourself.

Focused on the past experiences

Much of what happens in your internal conversations is based on past reflections. You often think about what you used to be compared to what you are today or what you could become in the future. These reflections focus more on past experiences than on your current situation or future goals. The challenge of pursuing future goals is rooted in the confidence (or lack of it) shaped by your past experiences.

Breaking the ties that bind you to your past is a real but a worthy journey to be on. Not all past experiences are unpleasant. And not all are for letting go and not including in your micro conversations. The goal is to change the tone of the conversation from being past focused. There is a difference in how you say something and the directional point of view it takes. If you are saying "I was really good at public speaking in high school," the tone is past focused, versus, "Public speaking is something I can do well. I even had some experience with it in high school." The tone shifts from focusing on past achievements as a good public speaker to emphasizing current abilities and the evidence that supports it.

Another reflection of this is, "She never helps me around the house. I can't depend on her." Switching the conversation to say, "I want her to help around the house, but not sure it will happen because we haven't had success before." The past is part of the conversation, but it is not the focus of it. The focus is on what is desired, "help around the house," and the past reflection is of what needs to be worked on.

Working to have your micro conversations to not be grounded in the past requires some work. Subtle things like this influence how you experience different situations. It creates a mood. It is the atmosphere around what you are doing in the moment. You want to make sure you are creating an atmosphere that is supporting the direction you want to go in, for the topic at hand.

Build on the image you have created

In so many ways, you can build up a perspective around what other people think about you. Opinions based on a look they have given you. An encounter where they dismissed your ideas. The lack of availability at a time when you needed them. It can be a single incident or multiple ones. In whatever the moment was, you started to give conversation to it.

You start to craft the story using details you remember from the situation. You add a point of view and an outcome. This conversation becomes the truth you live by when it comes to this individual in the future. Despite what they do or say moving forward, they are known by the things you have given conversations to.

Remember, these conversations work towards painting an image that is positive or negative. Let's consider some examples of this. Maybe you have been invited to an event. There are people you know and many you do not know. You make your efforts to mix and mingle. As you meet and greet people, you see those who are polite in conversations.

There are some who may offer a brief greeting before they are off to talk to the next person. Each encounter you are likely to walk off with a point of view of them, but also what you think is their interpretation of you—saying things like, "I don't think they thought I knew what I was talking about." Or, "I think she really connected with me." Or possibly, "The way he looked at me, I think he might like me." Or maybe even, "See how quickly she dismissed me."

Each individual comment you make to yourself is small and often easily ignored. You don't usually give much importance to a single micro conversation. The impact is not in the individual ones; it is in the summary of them. If you have enough micro conversations about one individual or enough from the collective group, it highlights the experience for you. The conversation becomes "I enjoyed myself. Everyone is so friendly and I think we all hit it off" or "I had nothing in common with anyone here. It was uncomfortable, and I felt like I didn't belong."

These micro conversations help you make decisions about future interactions with the people involved in your thoughts. They can also influence whether you choose to attend events and how engaged you will be. Being aware of these inner dialogues helps you understand what shapes your experiences with others and how you present yourself in different situations.

Your life situations

The behind-the-scenes conversation you have about your life happens throughout the day in little intervals. You will be at work and say something like, "Is this what my life will always look like?" Or maybe you are cooking dinner and say, "My life is exhausting." This micro conversation can be a one-liner, but has a ripple effect in triggering memories, other thoughts, and feelings. A simple statement leads to other self-describing points of view about your life at hand and the future outcomes you predict to be a part of your reality.

Micro conversations about your life can have an either or perspective. Your conversations lie on one extreme or the other. These conversations carry strong emotional ties to the past, present, and future. When you are having these types of conversations, whether intentional or not, they are weighted in how you experience them.

You can feel inspired by your micro conversations or uninspired. The tone of the conversation can place you in a position to dream of what can be or leave you doubting the possibilities. Your life experiences can be shaped in little intervals that are the behind-the-scenes messages to making decisions.

Inspired versus uninspired

To accomplish things in life, you need the motivation to go out and make them happen. To be encouraged that these things are possible. You will go out into the world and seek family, friends, and co-workers to have conversations that you hope will motivate you to take action. You will pick up a book seeking insight into what you can do differently to bring about change. Maybe that is the reason you are reading this book. And these options are relevant and helpful. But your internal conversation has to grab a hold of it in order to create the effect you are looking for.

Say, for instance, you are having coffee with a trusted friend. You guys are talking about your significant others. You share some hardships you are having in your relationship. Your friend is sympathetic to what you are dealing with and offers some words of hope. You, at that moment, are feeling inspired to keep working on the relationship. This is great. You had a micro conversation that had an impact towards your goal. A healthier relationship. You are feeling inspired.

What happens when you get home and the problems you face are still there? The default of uninspired conversations is triggered. Your micro conversations become about everything that is wrong and shifted from the moment of hope just gained in the conversation with your friend. The value of the conversation is in the power of the words your friend provided you. Now the shift comes in transitioning them into your own micro conversation. To put them on repeat in your conversation to yourself.

To be inspired in your micro conversations is to fuel them with words that reflect the change you are working towards. Allow room for the work you're doing to create change. To place focus on what is good versus what is challenging. These brief moments you can give yourself with consistency sets the space of being inspired. Imagine creating the perfect ambience in a room. You might light a candle, dim the lights, and play some soft music. The things you have done set the mood of the room. It helps someone walking into that space know what the intentions you have for the space created. An inspired space promotes what you want to happen there. Once you create the space, those present can take the cue and proceed with what you intended to be done within the space. Changing the words in your micro conversation can support creating an inspired space as well.

Dreamer versus doubter

There is another theme that your conversations fall under on a regular basis. It is one that is focused on dreaming versus doubting. A conversational tone filled with words that showcase the dreams and desire you have. Or centered on all the possibilities that keep it from happening.

Personality does drives some of this, while experiences shape the rest. It is important to look at what you are saying to yourself from a place of how it is serving you. Is it helping achieve the desired outcome or is it blocking your progress? Depending on where you are looking to go on the topic at hand is where your challenge lies in changing up these micro conversations.

Dreaming micro conversations are not about a fairy tale you tell yourself that is unobtainable. Not to say there are not moments of this. But dreaming conversation is about highlighting a desired outcome. It is in saying, "I look forward to a healthy relationship," "The job promotion is going to open up so many more professional opportunities," "I am looking forward to the day I get to travel more". These statements are painting a picture of what is possible. What you want your life to have.

Doubter conversations typically highlight the obstacles. They focus on what will make something unlikely to achieve. Things like "There are three others up for the promotion, not sure of my odds," "Traveling is something I wish could happen, but there is always so much work to be done. Not sure of when it is going to happen," "A healthy relationship would be nice, but we have so much baggage, not sure how we would get there." Often, when these conversations occur, it's not that you intentionally focus on the challenges. Unfortunately, when they are happening, you draw yourself to focus on the challenges, not the possibilities.

Learning more about these types of micro conversations helps you determine the work you need to do with them. Taking a moment to consider whether you are painting dreams or doubts can give you a next step challenge. Do you work on the parts that create doubt so they are no longer an obstacle? Or, do you make your dreams come true by taking action?

What others have

Internal micro conversations can also take on the focus of what others have. Sometimes it is in a comparative fashion, and at other times, it is just you being focused on what they have. Social media has amplified this type of conversation because of the increased access to what others promote is happening in their lives. This continues to increase the chatter about what they are doing, the relationships they have, the things they are purchasing. Acknowledging what others have can be either constructive or destructive.

The typical focus of micro conversations about what someone else has is about them only. It is focused on the benefits the other person is getting to have in life. What they are getting to experience. It is like singing their greatest hits and losing sight of yours. And before you dismiss the notion of this idea, think about it without defending your own point of view with this concept. For a moment, calm the micro conversation that is happening that says, "This can't be what I am doing." Understanding micro conversation is about recognizing the tone these small statements reflect back to you. And the impact of them as a collective, not in a single event. In a single event, they don't have to be a big thing. But when you get to a place where you can account for your conversations and there is a larger percent of time speaking about someone else, then that is cause to reevaluate what your micro conversations are focused on.

When having micro conversations that reflect what others have in their lives, be mindful not to let this overshadow the value of what you have. It's important to slow down and notice if your focus starts to shift away from your own worth.

Micro conversations that talk about what others have in terms of something you can strive for are useful. If you are having a conversation within that says "She was able to get her degree and land a great-paying job. It might be time for me to take the step and get mine too" or "I love seeing how in love they are. It gives me hope that kind of love is possible." The conversation reflects on what someone else has, but ties back to you in a way that inspires you.

Reflecting on what others have is a natural part of your day. It is easy to see something and account for the person who has it. The effort is managing how the reflection influences on who you are, your mood, and your experiences.

Chapter Four

Identifying Your Conversational Style

The topic of your micro conversation directs your focus to what captures your attention in the moment. How you present this information shapes your perspective. Imagine times when you are watching TV, perhaps the news. The news anchor delivers details about a story, providing the relevant facts. However, as they report these details, they often interject their perspective. They might express concern about a situation, speculate about its future impact, or offer a hopeful outlook. These elements of their report tailor the perspective of the anchor, and in turn, influence the viewer.

In your micro conversations, it's important to notice not just how often you focus on a topic, but also how you talk about it. Your style of speaking reveals your perspective and shapes your thoughts and reactions. Here's how it works:

When you talk to yourself about something, you're not just listing facts. You're viewing and describing those facts from your own point of view, shaped by your feelings, past experiences, and beliefs. For example, if you're thinking about a tough project at school, you might see it as really hard or as a fun challenge, depending on your outlook. This view affects how you feel about the project and how you approach it.

Just like how a news anchor's perspective can influence viewers, your perspective in a micro conversation influences your own thoughts and reactions. When you talk about something with a certain tone or attitude, it shapes how you feel inside. If you always see situations negatively, you might find challenges everywhere. But seeing things positively can boost your confidence and motivation.

Your internal dialogue creates a feedback loop that reinforces your perspective. Telling yourself, "I can handle this," builds resilience and readiness to tackle challenges. If your internal conversation says, "This is too hard," you might feel overwhelmed and less capable. This loop affects your mindset, behavior, and outcomes.

How you talk to yourself often shows up in how you talk to others. If your inner conversations are positive and helpful, you'll probably speak to others in a supportive way, too. This can improve your relationships and help create a positive environment around you.

By paying attention to what you talk about and how you talk about it in your micro conversations, you can see how they shape your actions and reactions. This understanding helps you manage your thoughts better and interact more positively with others. The goal is to create supportive micro conversations that help you grow and feel good, leading to a more positive approach to life's challenges.

In this chapter, we will dive deeper into understanding your internal micro conversations, identifying patterns, and learning how to use them to your advantage.

Worst-case/Best-case scenarios

There may be some other versions of how you might paint perspective in your micro conversation. For now, the focus will be on some general perspectives as describing information from a best-case/worst-case point of view.

In this version of your micro conversations, you take on giving the information in a way that highlights from potential outcomes. The conversation may be presented as "He is going to come in here late and tell me all the reasons he is late. It's going to turn into a big argument and I will look like the bad guy." This conversation lingers in your thoughts as you wait for his arrival home. Before either of you can open your mouth to address the subject of his late arrival, you have already described the event in a worst-case scenario. Your experience of your situation has already taken life before the other person could present any feedback from their actual events of the day.

These micro conversations can also take the perspective of a best-case scenario where you might say, "Today I have so much to do. But once I get it all done, the weekend will be free for me to relax and do nothing." The fact presented is you have a lot to accomplish. Completing the task will result in a relaxing weekend for you. The focus is not on the list of things to do, but on the restful weekend. This micro conversation could have looked like "I am already exhausted just looking at my to-do list. I don't even know if I can get it all done." This one might seem a little more familiar. In this, the outcome painted was one of exhaustion and disappointment that the list could even be completed.

Both examples show how internal conversations can shape your experience before you even start your to-do list. These micro conversations help set you up for the kind of experience you want to have.

Problem solver versus problem finder

This perspective looks at what you talk about in your micro conversations. These internal talks either try to find solutions to a problem or describe the obstacles you might face. "Problem solver" micro conversations are about brainstorming ways to improve a situation and planning how to get things done. When you talk to others, it's important to think about what can be achieved and to imagine positive outcomes.

Being a problem solver can keep you from being stuck on the problem. It can allow you to have conversations that support action towards your resolution. Your conversations can include statements like, "I know I can get through this . . . all I have to do is ___" or "My kid is having some challenges, but if she just ___ then I know it will work out." Your conversation can give hope. And it can give direction. It's important to consider the perspective of others when your solution could affect them.

Presenting information from a problem-finder perspective does not have to be seen as bad. Even though the nature of a problem finder is to find and talk about the things that are wrong in a situation, it does not mean it cannot be useful. A problem finder looks at the topic and speaks to the challenges to be addressed. There is little to no attention given to solutions. With this approach, you could present things like, "I don't have enough experience to be considered for that job." "Others are better looking than me. That is why I can't get a date." "In order to even have a chance, I would need to _____." You can see the situation for all the things that would need to be done or the things that keep it from being possible.

Being a problem finder can be beneficial in your micro conversations if you use it to identify areas for improvement and take action. For instance, if you think, "If I want to be successful in my relationship, I need to __," and then you actively work on those traits, this mindset shifts from highlighting obstacles to fostering actionable steps for improvement. This approach turns challenges into opportunities for growth.

The key is to understand both perspectives and not limit yourself to just the conversation. It is in creating a resource, as well as not stopping at what you are saying within, but being available to hear others' insights.

Wishful thinker

I wish I may; I wish I might. That magical place of thinking that creates a bubble where only the what's possible is seen. Wishful thinking primarily influences micro conversations to be influenced by what is desired. This differs slightly from thinking about what is possible. At times, you may have a desire, but struggle to see the path to attain it. Say your conversations are "I am going to marry a famous person and I won't ever have to stress about money again." While both parts of the statement are possible. You could marry a famous person and you could find yourself one day not stressing about money. The things that would line you up for either are not acknowledged in this conversation.

Conversations centered around wishful thinking can serve as a valuable escape from daily problems or traumatic experiences. They offer a safe space to reset and gain a sense of relief. A micro conversation like "I can see myself on a beach in Hawaii, relaxed, without a care in the world." This would be a wishful thinking conversation if there is no money saved in the bank, no vacation time from work, or no fear of flying. The value of this type of conversation is in creating a picture that is motivating enough to change your circumstances. To have a refreshing image of what it could be to relax, even though right now you may not be able to.

The idea of these micro conversation is in the imagery of something that is a stretch from present circumstances. The goal is not to limit yourself so much into these conversations that you set yourself up for disappointment. Disappointment that comes from not recognizing the work it takes to achieve the desired goal.

Absent-minded thinking

Your conversations within are your thoughts. Recognizing your thoughts as micro conversations is to give space to acknowledging that you are responding in some way to those thoughts. The days are filled with lots of information that can flood you at any moment. How you filter the information can sometimes show up in the way you are considering the information at any moment. It can be in forgetfulness, distraction, or being preoccupied. Having a lot to say, but saying a little.

Finding yourself in this type of conversation isn't about focusing on just one thing you're saying. It is what you are saying doesn't follow a logical path for understanding. You can gain little insight from your disorganized message.

Consider being at work. Your flow of conversation could be "Ok, so I need to get started on this assignment. I also need to pick up some tomatoes at the store. I wonder if my daughter took her jacket. Oh yeah, this assignment will need to get done today. I have to complete these assessments and get them printed. Is it cold in here?" A lot was said in a small amount of time. The challenge is in what information to focus on. What are you saying in a moment that helps you understand what you need to take away from it?

These micro conversations are usually about the experiences they create for you. They can make you feel overwhelmed by all the tasks you need to complete. This makes it hard to be fully engaged in conversations with others because your internal dialogue is always running.

It's tough to share information with someone else when your internal thoughts are jumbled and random. Sometimes these mixed-up conversations are rare and happen because of specific events. Other times, they can become a regular habit. No matter the cause, taking time to sort out your micro conversations helps you find the useful details to share clearly.

Your way of talking is an important tool for managing your micro conversations. When you know how you present information, you can better understand the responses you get. Your mood and actions are partly shaped by these internal talks. Changing how you share information can greatly affect your experiences and can also change how others respond to you.

Section 3

Transforming
Micro Conversations

Chapter Five

Transforming Your Internal Dialogues

It's easy to get lost in what you are talking about when you are passionate about it. You want to convey a message that holds significance. It's easy to escape into your head with endless thoughts and theories on the things that are happening. Before you know it, you have a whole storyline mapped out. Everything you have said completely convinced you. You have a whole monologue discussion for an audience of one.

The monologue conversation you have for the audience of one has now become the scripted version you will later communicate to others. Your version becomes the version you stand by and the version others will either have to accept or challenge you on.

When it comes time to change this internal dialogue, it's important to look at the specific parts that shape your thoughts. This means figuring out the key themes or negative patterns that keep coming up. By understanding these parts, you can replace unhelpful thoughts with better ones. This will lead to a healthier and more productive way of thinking.

What you say . . .

So many words. So many thoughts. So many opinions. A lot of understanding and perspective gets lost in the words that make up your micro conversations. What you are saying to yourself matters. And if you want to have micro conversations, that will support the results you desire. Working on what you say is going to be a key part of change.

Let's consider some examples of this. Maybe the topic in your conversation surrounds your work environment. At this time, your conversation is, "Today is going to be a long day. I have so much going on. I just know I will not get all done. I can already hear my supervisor telling me what I need to do differently. I wish I could just stay home, but it would be there when I get back. I can't wait for this day to be over." This conversation just sounds exhausting. It has already set the tone for the day and you haven't even walked out the door of your home. In these words, you have fueled your focus on everything wrong and challenging to your day. Your words have created an experience that shapes the exhaustion you feel prior to starting any task.

Here are some changes to the word choice. Same topic, different words. "There is a lot I need to get done today. I think if I take care of the reports before the meeting and then after the meeting, it will just be kind of a to-do list of things to take care. I know it is better to have a plan in mind. That way, my supervisor can't say anything to me. I think after work today, I will have truly earned to binge on my show with no distraction." The conversation was still a full day of work and anticipation of what the supervisor might try to do. But instead of the words focusing on the dread of the day, there was strategy. The words portrayed a plan to address the workload. The words even gave a way to wind down after the day was done. This conversation sets you up to walk out the door, motivated to get things done.

It requires work and effort to change your word choice, but this approach gives you one example of how it can influence where your energy and mood go.

How about the monologue that has to do with a relationship experience? Maybe you must address some parenting with your kid. The conversation within sounds like, "I am so tired of always having to tell her to clean up her room and do her work. By now, she should know better. It makes no sense that we still must have this conversation. I don't know if anything is going to get her on track." The words here support hopelessness and frustration. It already sets the tone for no progress to be made from the conversation. The challenge with these words is they can be valid acknowledgements. There is history that provides evidence to support the things you're saying. The reason for the rewrite is how it affects the outcome you would like to have. You don't really want your daughter to dismiss the value of cleaning up. You want your conversation with your child to spark change. Therefore, you should aim to speak words that support what you want to achieve rather than those that undermine your goals.

A rewrite might be, "I know I need to have this conversation, but I really want her to understand why it is important to clean up and do her work. This is something I know if she could just get better at, it would make things easier. I have to believe that something is going to help her get it." Here, you can still validate your feelings with your words. It conveys both concern and a desire for improvement. This phrasing allows you to express your wish for her well-being while maintaining a hopeful outlook for the future.

Your word choice influences your mood and your action. Being more intentional with your words helps keep both you and your listener engaged in the conversation. This approach ensures clarity and focus throughout your discussion. It also helps with what message is taken away from the conversation.

How you say it . . .

Your words matter, and so does how you serve them up. Has someone ever invited you to eat something new? You are told you are going to love it. That it has so much flavor. Then the plate of this amazing food is set before you and you pause. The pause is what you are seeing is not something you would want to eat. Its visual representation does not promote you taking a bite. Despite the selling points on how incredible it tastes, you can't get past what your eyes see. Because presentation matters.

Presentation is how you say something. It is the picture that is painted with your words. The feelings that are elicited by what you say. When you speak, you create an experience for yourself. You can say something is a compliment, but if it is not experienced as a compliment, it is not a compliment.

Consider saying, "This wasn't too bad; it could have been worse," or "I only made a couple of mistakes, so it's not as bad as before." While these words suggest you made some progress, they don't fully capture the picture of improvement. There is a sense of hesitancy on whether to be proud or judgmental. A reframe of this could be, "This was better than I have ever done." Or "I have made so much improvement." Both examples, while only subtle changes in how the information was represented, shifted the experience of hearing the words. These examples celebrate the growth with certainty that growth happened. Its emphasis is on what is better from a place of confidence. Which experience would you rather have for yourself? One that leaves you proud of what has happened or feeling uncertain about the progress made.

How you say something should also be clear in its message. If what you say does not clearly reflect where you stand on a topic, then your experience goes from focusing on the topic, to the confusion of how you have presented the topic.

What this looks like is, "I really want to go on vacation, but I know I need to save money. I even looked up the cost of the trip to see how much it would be." Here, two messages are presented. One that promotes travel and the other saving money.

You have presented yourself with a conflict. The conversation tends to further focus on the choice of do you travel or do you save money. What you really wanted the conversation to focus on was can I make a vacation happen. A shift in presentation might look like, "It's time for me to have a vacation. I have to create a budget for the trip I would like to go on." Here, all the focus is on making the trip happen, but you can also accommodate the reality of your budget. Saying this to yourself allows for hope that the vacation is possible as well as gives a step to make it happen. You want to talk in a way that supports the outcome you desire.

Your intentions in conversations

You ever have those moments when you stop talking and wonder what was the point I was trying to make? Or when you are talking with someone else and they have a glazed look in their eyes like they're lost? Words become just words when the message is unclear. Even more. Words are just words when you don't know what you want to come out of them.

Taking time to slow down and know what you want on the other side of your conversation is the start of a good conversation. "Ask yourself, do my words help me achieve the results I want? What should I be saying to reach my goals? Do I want to be healthier? Are my words supporting me to be healthier? Do I want to be a better spouse? Are my words creating a space for me to be a better spouse? Do I want to be a better leader? Are my words an example of my leadership?

It's not just about a conversation filled with one-liner affirmations, saying "You are Smart. You are Bold. You are a Leader." Your micro conversations illustrate an image of what it looks like. "Every day I learn ways to become a better leader. I thrive in the place of growth and leadership. In everything I do, I put forth my best, to bring about the best in others." Which of these ways of communicating shifted you to just reading them? Which of these influenced you to see an image of what it would be like to take action?

The one-liner might highlight a trait. The effectiveness comes in transporting you to a place of imagery. Supporting the experiential side of what you say. In order to create this kind of dialogue, you must understand what you want on the other side of your words.

What does this look like in negative situations, like an unhealthy marriage? Instead of saying, "I am struggling to stay in this marriage," you can say, "I am finding new ways to handle the things happening in my marriage." Your conversation should be honest about your situation. Your internal conversation can be a safe place for reflection. It's important that your micro conversation acknowledges your true experience while also creating a space to support a positive and helpful outlook.

Maybe the situation is a problematic work environment. Changing from "I really don't want to work today. It's just going to be the same thing it always is" to "Today I am going to find something I can be proud of about myself." The first statement supports seeing the worst of what the day offers. The second sets the direction to look for something good in the day. This doesn't mean there won't be things you dislike in your day. The conversation will help you stay focused on what you want to achieve throughout your day.

Knowing your intentions for what you say helps you to choose your words to align with the desired outcomes. This takes slowing down to think about what you want. Learning that what you set your focus on is what you find. This is a way to be genuine about your experience without it having to set a negative tone. A way to talk about traits you used to excel in rather than focusing on what you've lost. Consider your outcome first, then figure out the words of your conversation.

What is the conversation based on . . . fact or fiction

There are times the conversations that run through your mind get muddied between the details and your interpretation of the details. Your internal micro conversations are a place where you work out your thoughts and opinions regarding your experience. You consider your experience from a solo perspective. Yours! The only feedback given is Yours. The only description of the experience is Yours. There is no one to disagree with you. There is no one to challenge the facts. There is no one to give additional insights from others' perspectives. This can become tricky if you don't allow an opportunity for discussion to gain perspective on the experience from someone else. This is where it gets muddy.

At some point, your information on an experience becomes intertwined with the facts. You can have micro conversations recapping things as though they were a part of the original experience. You can assign people's intentions as fact because you talked about them so often with yourself. This becomes even more confusing when your conversation focuses on yourself, because you would think you are the best person to describe who you are. And that is not always the case.

Let's consider some examples of both. First, when you have an internal micro conversation about an experience.

You might say, "The event I went to last night was filled with lots of people. I talked to several people, but no one was interested in what I had to say. It was such a waste of my time being there." This conversation seems simple enough. It gives a reflection of you personal experience.

If we were to take a moment to challenge the version of this experience with others, we might find that the conversations with the people mentioned last for thirty minutes or more. That from the other people's point of view, they stayed talking in the conversation because you were making valid points. The conversation was interesting, but not related to the event, so engagement was limited because of the need to refocus.

Upon further investigation, it was found that you actually received a new job assignment, made a new friend, or got an invitation to a future event. The challenge arises when you don't consider perspectives beyond your own, causing your viewpoint to be seen as the only reality.

It becomes the one you reference with others when you recap this experience. This can happen with so many things like discussions with your family, trips you go on, presentations at work or school. At some point, to establish if your conversation is based on fact or fiction, you need additional input. You also have to be in a place of willingness to reconsider your details if the additional input makes your version inaccurate.

Now let's consider an example when the subject of your micro conversation is interpreting yourself. The conversations might sound like "I am not a good parent. I can't seem to get my kid to school on time. My child can't make friends. I don't know what I am doing." This conversation is a personal reflection that is limited in your recap.

If the focus is only on what you do wrong or does not give space to effort. Your details are muddied by fiction. If we consider additional facts, the days that your kid is late are related to things out of your control like traffic, they spilled on their clothes and needed to change; the alarm didn't go off, or any of the other countless things that might occur in a morning routine. Should that define your ability to be a good parent?

Your kid might not be making friends. How much control do you have in making friends for them? If you were to get additional perspectives, would you find that you often encourage your child, practice ways to make friends, have talked to the teacher, arrange play options with your friends' children? Would these be better details to determine how you operate as a parent?

Conversations that are limited to your point of view don't allow room for others' feedback, making it hard to understand different details. This can lead to confusion where your version of events feels like the only truth. To change this, try getting feedback from others. Focus on the facts of the event instead of your interpretation. Listen to others' opinions directly from them. Look beyond the immediate moment to see more outcomes from the experience. This approach helps create a clearer, more accurate conversation.

Your micro conversation is a place of reference. You want to get the facts straight.

Shifting your focus on how you consider past experiences

The past has a lot that lives in it. In the present, the past is revisited. The past shows up often to influence the future. If the past shows up to do so much in your life, wouldn't you say it is relevant to alter how it affects you?

Addressing your internal conversations about past experiences involves using what you've learned from the past to help you now and in the future. Focus on the lessons and positive outcomes that can guide you. It's important to decide what memories are helpful to talk about and which ones are not worth repeating. This helps you avoid dwelling on negative thoughts and keeps your internal dialogue supportive and positive. By doing this, you can create a balanced view of your past that helps you grow and maintain well-being.

It's simple to have your micro conversations reflect details on an event that happens. To account for where you were, what happened, and how you responded. The effort to shift your focus is not on altering the details as much as it is the perspective. Switching your focus to things like what you learned from an experience, the traits you used to get through it, or the traits that you have learned because of it. Maybe it is the people you meet or let go of. Working on the perspective of these past experiences involves finding the resources that will help you create the next chapter in your life.

Let's explore some examples of this. Maybe as a child, your parents went through a messy divorce. Your micro conversations could be "My parents were always yelling and in arguments before they were divorced. It was hard to hear. I always wished they would just stop." These are relevant memories. They acknowledge what it was like growing up with your parents before divorce.

The conversations that stay in this focus maintain the hardship and maybe some negativity to marriage. Shifting the focus of these conversations to something like, "I am glad I met ___. They have been my anchor through some difficult times." Or "My parents' relationship has taught me the value of finding someone I can communicate with." The past focus is not on the details of what happened, but a resource you have gained because of it.

How about school experiences? Maybe in your younger years, you were not a very good student in terms of the grades you received. A micro conversation might look like, "I have never been a good student. I always received the bare minimum grade to get by. My parents would always seem so disappointed. I have no desire to go through that again."

Think about it. If you were up for a promotion and you were required to get a certification, do you pass up on that promotion because your view of your school experience is negative? Are you motivated to go after the certification when you are coming from a place that you are not good in an educational setting?

Revising this conversation becomes relevant in order for it to not be a roadblock. The revision could look like, "I have had to work harder at school than others. I have learned the value of pushing myself to make things happen. Even though my grades weren't the best, I made it through." This conversation still captures that school was difficult and grades were not good.

The difference is in what traits it promoted. It promotes that hardships are not a place of failure, but endurance. It reflects a journey of overcoming and persistence, which reinforces the value of pursuing future educational experiences.

Reshaping these conversations requires some work. And there are past experiences that may require some healing along the way. The effort is directed towards shaping your future experiences. It aims to influence how your past affects your present and future.

Chapter Six

Self-Talk and Self-Perception: Why Your Words Matter

Your micro conversations are like short stories you create. When you talk to yourself or others, you are telling a narrative. This narrative forms an image and describes the facts related to that image. What you say matters, even if it seems small at the moment. These conversations can become important reference points in the future.

Understanding micro conversations involves examining how they function and learning how to change the way you engage in them. It's essential to think about the experiences that result from these conversations. These small talks can influence how you see things and help you decide what will happen next. They also guide others by linking different stories together. Knowing how you have these conversations helps you manage their impact on you.

When you talk to yourself, you are reinforcing your beliefs and perspectives. This internal dialogue can either support your growth or hold you back. For instance, if you tell yourself, "I can handle this challenge," you are building confidence and resilience. On the other hand, if you say, "This is too hard for me," you might feel defeated before you even start.

When you talk to others, your micro conversations help shape how they see you and your shared experiences. If you often talk about your struggles without mentioning your successes, people might think you're always having a hard time. But if you share both your challenges and achievements, it gives a more balanced view and can inspire others.

By being aware of your micro conversations, you can choose words that encourage positive outcomes. This means focusing on solutions rather than just problems and thinking about the bigger picture of your experiences. When you communicate well, you create a supportive environment for yourself and those around you. This thoughtful way of talking helps you build stronger relationships and handle life's challenges more easily.

Influences your current experiences

A single comment. The one thing someone says that stands out among all the other words and topics. That single remark that takes you back in time. The one phrase that touches your heart. At a moment's notice, a conversation can shift your experience. Words have power. To discover a little more of their influence, let's look at three areas: mood, energy, and actions.

Take the mood to start off. Say you are in a pleasant mood. Pretty relaxed day watching your favorite show come on TV. A commercial comes on talking about purchasing a home. It lasts about 20 seconds, but you spend the next 20 minutes having an internal conversation. You are saying things like, "I want to buy a house. I need to really get to saving money. It would be easier if I made more money. Renting has become so expensive. I am not sure when I will purchase. Ugh, I don't know where to begin."

These comments may happen back to back or trickle here and there for the next few minutes. Every time one shows up, the mood shifts to stress, frustration, concern. The effects are temporary for the moment it shows up. Or it may be lingering.

You ever have that moment when you are in your own head, considering something, and someone walks in? They start talking and you react in a way that shows irritation. That person is confused by your reaction because it does not seem to match the topic they are addressing. This is when the mood experienced by the internal conversation influences you more than an external one.

Energy is another space where conversations can shift your experience. Consider times where you have been in conversation with someone. There are people who just in their style of communication can be draining. It could be in the tone of voice they speak. It could be a topic of discussion. Whatever the factors are, you seem to walk away more often than not from a conversation with them, feeling zapped of energy.

How can words shift the energy of how you feel? Words act as triggers. They prompt additional internal conversations and references you hold within. They can be a trigger to historical experiences. Or bring you to a place of an anticipated future. You ever have that moment when someone starts into a conversation where you say to yourself, "Here we go again." That reflection is loaded with meaning. It is the meaning associated with the response that influences your energy shift. You are no longer just responding to the here and now experience, but also to whatever experience connected to the trigger.

Energy shifts can be shown in changes in your tone, body language, and engagement levels. Consider for a minute a conversation you might have with yourself. In this conversation, you are saying, "This is going to be a long day. I have so much to get done; I don't even know where to begin."

The anticipation of what is coming can shift your energy to feeling drained. There is exhaustion in just considering the task of the day and you haven't even gotten started. By becoming more mindful of these simple conversations, you gain the ability to create a different experience. To say "I have a lot to accomplish, but oh how sweet the rest will feel when it is all done," the anticipation becomes hopeful or encouragement of what you want to feel. It does not take away from the reality of what you need to do, but your focus is on something that does not take your energy level down.

Energy and mood shifts with micro conversation influence your actions as well. Think about basketball for a minute. The game is broken down in four quarters with a half-time break in the middle. The coach is given the option to call timeouts throughout the game. What typically happens in these breaks? There is some level of rest that can occur for the players. But that is not the only use of these breaks.

What also happens in these moments is the coach has an opportunity to talk to the player or players. The conversations may be about a play they want them to run, what they what them to pay attention to, what to watch out for in the other players, or it may be accountability to how they are playing. Whatever is said in these brief moments influences how the player returns to the court and performs.

Well, coaching conversations happen not only in the sporting industries. There are directors in movies, executive coaches in the business worlds, and teachers in the classrooms. And then there are also you and the people in your life. The micro conversation that influence action or sometimes inaction may sound like "You are really good at keeping things organized" (this supports maintenance of a habit reflected by someone else) or "You will never be good at ___" (can either influence you to work harder to prove this wrong or cause you to stop because you consider its truth).

This can also happen in subtle conversations, like when someone says, "It's hard to talk to you about things. I just wish it was easier to open up to you." These words might lead to actions like pulling away, talking less, or avoiding the person. The speaker is sharing their feelings, but without more information or clear expectations, the listener has to guess what the speaker means.

Micro conversations that influence your actions come in many shapes and forms. The key is to notice how these conversations are affecting you. Then, take the time to change the ones that are not supporting the experiences you want to have.

Influences your future experiences

The conversations that you have now can linger into your future. They can set the tone for future events well before you even get there. Sometimes, these words become a script that you invest energy and effort into maintaining, even when they no longer reflect your circumstances. Awareness may be an overused word, but it applies to so much that we do and get out of life. Dedicate time to learn and grow from your experiences. To be more intentional about your future, you need to be more in tune with the conversations surrounding events in your life.

Let's break this thought down a little further. Think about when you were going through your early years of school. Go back to maybe third or fourth grade. The teachers had a point of view on what kind of student you were. They acknowledged this daily. With grades you would achieve on papers. Saying things like, "You did a great job. Keep this up." Or maybe it was "You could do better. You are not trying hard enough." Or any other variation of comments they could have made about your performance.

Maybe it was something more specific, like "Maybe writing isn't your strength; just do what you can," or "You're really good with numbers. You must love math."

These simple comments, whether positive or negative, can have an immediate effect and may also influence you in the future without you even realizing it.

For a moment, consider your high school years. Are there any perspectives from your early grade school teachers that you still held onto in high school? Did you focus more on your writing skills because the teachers before said you were a really good writer? Did you shy away from classes like math because you were deemed a poor math student in elementary school?

If the answer is yes, don't get caught up in how the teachers of your youth gave feedback. Those reflections at the moment they happened reflected the moment. People can only be so selective in their everyday conversations. The purpose of this book is not even to get critical or detailed about every conversation you have. It is a resource of unpacking the things that are influencing you when you are looking to do differently.

To understand how micro conversations affect your future experiences, think about the talks that have shaped how you see yourself and your abilities. These small conversations help form your expectations and give you an idea of what an experience will be like before it even happens. Reflect on times when someone, including yourself, has described what it would be like to do something or be someone. These talks can influence your actions and mindset.

When you dig deeper into the micro conversations that shape your future interactions, you'll find they can involve both people and situations. Think about your interactions with people for a moment. Have you ever had a coworker who always asks questions you don't want to answer? Or maybe you find yourself wasting time in conversations that wander into topics that aren't necessary.

Your internal dialogue often defaults to remembering past experiences to predict what will happen each time you meet this person. This means your reactions are already set based on these past conversations. While this internal dialogue might seem valid, it can limit how you handle the current situation. But if you become aware of this pattern, you can change how you react and create a better experience instead of just repeating old habits.

For example, if your micro conversation is "Here she goes. She always talks about everyone and what they are doing. I really don't care, but I always get sucked in." If you can take the time to notice this conversation, then you can change your experience. You can approach it in a couple of different ways. You can put a time limit on the conversation informing that person in the beginning you cannot talk long. Or you can let them know your desired topic to talk about at that moment. The goal is to express your need based on what you became aware of in your micro conversations.

This can happen with situations as well. You can talk with someone or yourself about a situation that is upcoming. Your conversation is loaded with details about what to expect. Sometimes, this can be a helpful resource. If your conversations are aimed at planning and preparation to achieve a desired outcome, the goal is not to label them based on past experiences. Instead, focus on the potential for success and the steps needed to reach your goals. This means avoiding assumptions that things will turn out as they have before and instead, shaping your conversations to support your goals and desired results.

This understanding starts with recognizing what influences you and your circumstances. Initially, these conversations seem simple, usually reflecting on your current situation. However, the challenge is that they can carry over from that moment of reflection, affecting future experiences. Mastering the ability to gauge your conversations helps you manage their impact on your future more effectively. The more you can control and shape these internal dialogues, the better you can support positive outcomes.

Influences your feedback to others

You have an opinion. And this opinion comes from somewhere. This opinion can carry an intensity that strengthens or weakens on the fuel it is given. The fuel is the conversations on the topic.

Micro conversations shape how you respond to others and to yourself. Repeating a topic can often strengthen your viewpoint. In relationships, one challenge is focusing on a problem from just one perspective.

For example, one spouse might repeatedly talk about what the other did wrong and why they think it happened. Without exploring this issue further, this narrow view can influence how they continue to respond to their spouse's actions. It can also affect how they advise friends about similar situations, adding doubt about relationships based on their own experiences.

Your feedback can be a valuable resource for others. Sharing your experiences can help guide others along a supported path, strengthening their own journeys. However, as emphasized throughout this book, it is important to be aware of the source of your feedback. Understanding where it comes from is essential.

Interestingly enough, your feedback can become an expert account of how to do things. This can happen because of your position with the person you are giving feedback to. Such as a parent, supervisor, or teacher. Or the person trusts you would only give them information that was good for them to hear, information that is supportive, based on their needs. Therefore, understanding the conversational focus of your micro conversation is important.

Before you provide feedback, check your own personal bias. You can have your opinion. But at the end of the day, it is yours that you have built up from your experience. It may or may not be accurate for the person you are giving feedback to.

Understand your motive. Giving feedback is not always resourceful to give. Sometimes feedback is given without giving space to the benefit of the one you are giving it to. At times, it comes from a place of personal need to share your opinion. If your motive is not about supporting the need of the person you are sharing it with, then it may be relevant to keep your opinion.

Recognize that your feedback has an impact. This impact comes from your personal conviction and the commitment you have to your perspective, which results from your micro conversation experiences. Your strong desire for others to see things from your point of view can sometimes helpful, but it can also be harmful. The way you regulate yourself and their experience is in slowing down to recognize what is happening.

Taking the initiative to pay attention to where your feedback is coming from can go a long way.

Section 4

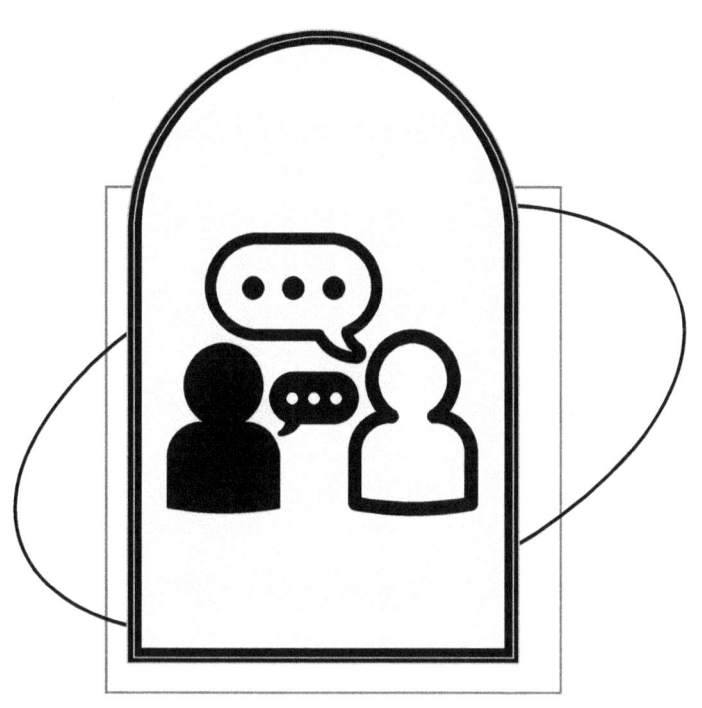

Applying
Micro Conversations
in Daily Life

Chapter Seven

Understanding Your External Conversations

Until now, we've focused on your internal conversations. We've looked at how you talk to yourself, how often these conversations happen, and their bigger impact. But now, let's think about another part: the micro conversations you have with others.

Let's revisit what a micro conversation is. These are the simple, frequent talks you have about a topic. It's not about the length of each conversation, but the pattern and tone that matter for future interactions. To illustrate this, think about a time when someone finished your sentence or predicted what you were going to say. How can they do this?

It stems from these micro conversations. You've discussed a point of view enough times that others pick up on it. Your responses can become automatic rather than thoughtful. This isn't necessarily good or bad, but it's important to recognize. If you need to change, understanding this helps. Making changes isn't always simple for others to accept, or even for yourself to acknowledge.

As we looker deeper into micro conversations with others, think about a few things. Consider who you're talking to about certain topics, whether the conversation is important, and if it's time to change how you talk about these things.

Recognizing Your Conversational Themes

Pay attention to what you often talk about with others to find the key themes in your conversations. Do you frequently discuss topics like school, family, hobbies, or news? Identifying these themes can show you what you focus on and how it affects your thoughts and feelings.

The micro conversations you have with others often show your unique style and viewpoint. Each interaction has a flow that you might not notice, but others might expect from you. For example, you might always start by talking about school before moving on to personal topics, or you might use jokes to make serious conversations lighter.

Understanding how you talk with others is important. It means knowing how you share information and how others react. Do you usually start the conversation, or do you prefer to listen first and then talk? Do you like to give a lot of details, or do you keep your points short and simple?

By looking at these patterns, you can understand how what you say and hear influences your conversations. This helps you improve your communication, making your conversations more effective and meaningful. It also shows you how talking with others affects your views and relationships.

If you're more aware of what you talk about, you'll understand your conversations better. Likewise, being mindful of your conversations helps you handle your interactions better. By recognizing the key topics and styles of your conversations, you can see how your words affect others and adjust your approach to create positive interactions. This mindfulness not only improves your relationships, but also helps you feel more confident and comfortable in social situations.

Externally Related vs. Personally Related

In considering the themes of your conversation, let's start from a place of what you typically talk about. Do your conversations usually focus on personal topics, or are they more about external matters like work? Why is this relevant you might ask? It is relevant for two things I want you to consider here: what you are giving energy and attention to and how it matters to you.

Your primary conversation shows what is taking up time and place in your life. Every time you talk about something, it takes up energy, emotion, and mind space. It is influencing the course of your day and your mood. When you wonder why you feel exhausted despite not doing much. Consider the topics of your day.

The other part of these micro conversations is sometimes it creates a false sense of importance. If you are spending your day complaining about work. While work may be important, is it more important than your children? How much time are you spending talking about them or to them? By tuning into your micro conversations, you are taking a moment to realize how they affect you and the others you are in conversation with.

There are times when one area of your life may need to dominate your conversational focus. For instance, if your family is going through some hardships, you might need to shift your focus from work to handle personal matters. Your conversations will revolve around acknowledging the situation and figuring out how to adjust and address things. On the other hand, you might be working on an important project that requires your attention before and after work hours. Or perhaps a significant change has occurred in your work environment that concerns you. This might increase the need to discuss work-related issues during your personal time.

Being aware of what you focus on in conversations helps you stay mindful of what's capturing your attention. Sometimes, you might be more interested in topics like politics, sports, or events outside your personal responsibilities. If you notice you're spending too much time on these subjects, you can work on balancing your conversations. By understanding how these topics affect you, you can better manage your mood and how available you are emotionally to others.

Future related vs. past related

The concept of future- versus past-related conversations has to do with where you relate most of your information to. Future conversations take the perspective of what you would like to accomplish. It can also be presented as "when this happens, then I ___." Future conversations are focused on things that haven't happened, which maintain a degree of uncertainty within the conversation. That uncertainty can lead to either hope or doubt. By becoming more mindful of your words, you can guide and influence their impact on you more effectively.

Past-related conversation present with historical information. They contain details of what once was, or what happened to you, or how something that happened made you feel. In these types of conversations, you stay anchored to a state of being that may not be supportive of your present day or what you would like your future to be. There is a time and place for both themed conversations. The repetitive parts of these conversations are what you want to be mindful of. This is where the impact of them as micro conversations begin to influence you.

Others focused vs. you focused

This next theme can be tricky to discuss. It focuses on who you believe is responsible for the things happening in your life. These conversations might be about past events, explaining why you feel a certain way, or based on your beliefs about certain topics. The main point of these conversations is to figure out where you think the responsibility lies.

Are you placing responsibility on yourself in the conversation, or on someone else? Remember, this isn't just about a single conversation. A onetime discussion focused on an individual only gives a snapshot of that moment. Considering who you focus on is necessary because it shapes the overall theme of your conversations and where responsibility is placed.

For example, when talking about things that happened in your childhood, you might share how you didn't have many friends and explain it was because you weren't very athletic, or maybe you were smart, and others didn't like you. In this case, you're placing the focus on yourself and how you influenced the situation.

On the other hand, you might describe how the other kids were mean or only wanted certain people in their group. Here, you're giving responsibility to others for the situation you experienced as a kid.

The goal here isn't to determine whether these points are true. It's to discuss the repetitive theme you find yourself in when talking about this situation.

When you focus mainly on one person, whether it's yourself or others, you limit your perspective to just that point of view. If you focus only on yourself, it's helpful to understand your strengths and areas for growth. However, it might also make you feel you should have had more control over the situation, which could be unfair to you.

If you focus too much on others, you miss the opportunity to reflect on what you could have done differently or on how you might grow in the future.

You want to give space to look at both your part and others. It's important to balance your conversations, giving place to the parts you might be missing. If you find yourself trending in one-directional conversations, try to shake it up and consider different perspectives. This way, you gain a more balanced understanding and can grow from the experience.

Roles you play

Looking at your conversations with others isn't always easy. It's simpler to keep doing what you have always done and to move through conversations without thinking about their impact. Or maybe we tell ourselves that because we're uncertain about what we'll find if we look deeper. But having this level of insight can bring simplicity and value. What is more draining is living with the results of our conversations and not understanding why we feel and think the way we do.

I am challenging you at this moment to see this truth or be reminded of why you started in this journey with me, because this next section is going to require a different level of honesty. To truly consider the role you are playing in your conversations with others, I may even sound like a broken record, but this is not about judgement but awareness. And with awareness comes the information that will support your growth. Support your healing. Support your change.

In thinking about the role you are playing in conversations, we are going to look at how you cast yourself into a conversation. This casted role is regarding what your part is, as it relates to how you deliver information to others.

First up in discussion is your role to inform others about what you need and how you are influenced by things. I am jumping right in to the hardest one of all first. You will notice yourself taking on this role if most of the conversation centers around what you need from others. Let's say someone starts a conversation with you about how hard their day has been. When it is your opportunity to express your thoughts, it will have little to nothing to do with what is going on for that person, and will shift to what is going on for you. This can be intentional and unintentional.

The unfortunate consistency in this role is that it doesn't give space to others in the conversation. One of the most challenging parts of a conversation is you are always going to be triggered to have a thought as it relates to you. Growth comes from knowing when, how, and if it's relevant to mention something at that moment. There is value in balancing out when you take on this role. It's not that the point you want to make doesn't matter. Instead, making sure it fits with the current conversation.

Another important aspect of conversations is the roles we take, like being an advice giver or a listener. Both roles are important, but problems can happen if they are mixed up. When you give feedback, you share your thoughts and feedback based on what the other person is saying. Advice givers usually focus on what to say about someone else's situation. They rarely reflect on the information. They listen mainly to find something to respond to.

A listener takes in information as it is given, without interpreting or reflecting on it. They value their role of simply being there to listen and may not focus on giving feedback. For them, listening itself is providing a valuable resource. Like being an advice giver, sometimes just listening is appropriate. However, problems can arise if the person talking needs more than just a listener. They might need feedback or advice, and that's when being only a listener can be a challenge.

In conversations, you might be known for focusing on the positive or the negative. By themselves, neither approach is bad. However, if you always stick to one, it can limit how you engage in conversations. These types of micro conversations can shape how you see yourself and how others see you. It's important to have a balance to show different sides of yourself.

Playing the role of giving positive feedback in conversations creates a supportive environment. This makes people see you as someone who is helpful and encouraging. Positive conversations focus on finding solutions, keeping things running smoothly, or seeing the best in a situation. While these are great qualities, they're not always what's needed. It can also be tough to always be expected to stay positive. In terms of micro conversations, understanding these roles helps you distinguish between what others expect from you and what is actually needed at any given moment.

Taking on the negative role can also be tough. Always pointing out what's wrong and what's not working can create its own kind of stress. Sharing this kind of feedback can be important because it shows where improvement is needed and helps people move past doing things the same old way. Negative feedback has its place and can be very useful. However, if it's the only way you communicate, it can be harmful. It's important to know when to give negative feedback based on what's needed in the conversation, not just as your usual way of talking.

Micro conversations, the roles you play in them, and the themes they follow give insight into your patterns. When you want to make changes, understanding your past roles helps you decide if they will support your new goals. Don't overlook the small lessons from these patterns.

Chapter Eight

Recognizing Barriers in Communication

C onversations should have a purpose, especially the ones you find worth repeating. There's often a relaxed nature when we talk to someone else. You come home after a busy day and start chatting with your family. When you arrive at work, you greet your co-workers. You might call a close friend. No matter the setting, your words flow naturally.

In this chapter, I don't want to take away from the natural flow of how you engage in conversations. Instead, I encourage you to be accountable for the conversations you have. While conversations might feel relaxed and informal, they still influence you. It is this influence that is beneficial to manage.

As I guide you through the importance of discussing these topics in conversations, I encourage you to be reflective with yourself. This isn't about criticism, but about gaining awareness. Understanding how micro conversations impact your day, mood, and actions helps you manage how you present yourself in any situation. Building this skill is very valuable for your well-being.

It's also important to think about why you talk about certain topics more than others. By looking at the reasons behind your choice of topics, you can find out what motivates, interests, or worries you. This deeper understanding can help you spot patterns and make better choices about what you talk about and why. This can lead to more meaningful and satisfying conversations that improve your well-being and relationships.

For example, if you often talk about work, it might show that you're looking for validation or dealing with job-related stress. On the other hand, if you frequently talk about your personal achievements, it could mean you want recognition and support from those around you. By examining your conversation topics more closely, you can understand your needs better and address them more effectively. This self-awareness not only improves your communication skills, but also helps you have more balanced and meaningful conversations.

Has your conversation topic become habits

Do you talk about a topic or situation just out of habit? Many of our conversations stem from repetition. Much of our daily lives operate on routine. You wake up in the morning and follow a set of activities to start your day. You go to work and again find yourself in a routine. Finally, you come home and engage in your usual evening activities. In many ways, this repetitiveness helps you function and get things done. Constantly adjusting to new things each day would require more mental and emotional effort.

When it comes to conversations, having some routine types of interactions can be helpful. For example, regularly checking in with co-workers can set limits on how long you chat before starting work tasks. Likewise, asking your kids how their day went and getting the usual "Good" response works for most daily interactions. These routine conversations help keep a sense of normalcy and structure in your life.

Reflecting on your habitual conversations is important because not all of them support your needs. Some routine conversations can keep you in a bad mood, while others might trap you in a cycle that you need to break. It's crucial to identify these patterns so you can make changes that better match your goals and well-being. This way, you can have conversations that help you feel better and reach your goals.

Let's talk about how to spot and change conversations that might need fixing. Instead of immediately picking specific conversations to change, start by looking at the situations you want to improve. For example, if you often feel irritated by midday, which then affects your afternoon meetings, think about the conversations you have earlier in the day. Do these talks make you feel better or worse? By understanding how these conversations affect you, you can start making changes to have a more positive day.

Ask yourself if you're having negative discussions with co-workers about job problems or venting about personal struggles. These patterns, including your own internal thoughts, can set a negative tone for the rest of your day. By thinking about these early conversations with others, you can find and change the ones that make you irritable, helping you create a more positive and productive mindset.

Once you figure out which conversations happen all the time, the next step is to change them on purpose. You might talk less to people who lead you into these unhelpful discussions. Focus on changing how you talk about certain topics, or decide not to engage in those conversations at all. If a regular conversation makes you feel bad and doesn't help you, it's time to make a change.

What about the habitual conversations where you always maintaining the same perspective? These are the ones where your point of view, feelings, and reactions stay unchanged. In fact, people close to you can predict what you'll say before you even say it. These habitual conversations can keep you stuck in a mindset or situation you may not want to be in.

Maybe it's the conversations you have about relationships where you always respond positively. You find it hard to see any negativity, so people expect you to say things like, "It's going to be okay; they are a really good person" or "Don't worry about it; you guys are good together." Your response is always reflective of a positive future. While this can sometimes be helpful, it might not always be the best approach. If you are responding out of habit, you might not be interpreting your conversation based on the specifics of the situation.

Habitual conversations can be helpful. But it's important to think about how effective they are by looking at their impact. You want your conversations to support the experiences you're trying to create. By being mindful of the impact of your habitual conversations, you can make adjustments to ensure they contribute positively to your overall well-being and personal growth.

Seeking solutions

Sometimes, the conversations you have are about finding solutions. This means sharing information in a way that invites others to give feedback. The goal is to gather helpful information about your current situation. Why is this important for micro conversations? Remember, micro conversations are about having the same type of talk repeatedly. If you are always looking for solutions on the same topic, the conversation should focus on finding a solution you can actually use.

When you're looking for solutions, it's important to focus on self-discovery. Are you talking about topics that make you feel insecure? For example, if you're always discussing your ability to speak up for yourself and constantly seeking ways to improve, but rarely or never put these solutions into action, the conversation stops being helpful.

Instead of finding solutions, it becomes more about high-lighting an ongoing struggle. This can make it harder to move forward, turning the conversation into an obstacle rather than a path to improvement.

When you challenge yourself to examine the conversations you have with others; the goal is to determine whether these conversations are productive and if you're truly getting what you need from them. If you find the answer is no, then it's time to change the conversation.

When you're having conversations to find solutions, they should naturally show progress. Each time you talk about the same topic, there should be some signs that things are getting better. If your "seeking solutions" conversations are working well, you'll bring up new insights and experiences in your discussions. For example, if you're working on speaking up for yourself and someone suggests practicing with a trusted person, the next time you discuss this topic, you should talk about how that practice went. Focus on your efforts and progress instead of starting from the problem again. This way, you can see how far you've come and what you've learned.

When you frequently discuss a topic to the point that it becomes a micro conversation, ensure it's helping you move forward, not keeping you stuck.

Venting as the focus

Who doesn't benefit from a good conversation to get things off their chest? Having a chat with someone you enjoy talking to is easy and refreshing. It might happen over your favorite drink, between work activities, or on your drive home. A venting conversation allows you to be heard and lets others know what's going on with you. So, what's the issue with venting conversations, you might ask? Aren't they helpful? My answer is yes. A good venting conversation every now and then can be very beneficial.

These types of conversations are a great way to feel heard. Sometimes, that's all we need—someone willing to listen to what's going on with us. No feedback is necessary, just good old-fashioned listening. Being heard can provide the support you need.

Let's think about how venting as a micro conversation can impact us. Imagine if every time you talked to someone, they only shared their problems and ended the conversation once they were done venting. If this sounds like you, don't be too hard on yourself. Instead, become aware of the experience it creates. When this type of conversation happens repeatedly, it leaves no room for other perspectives, reflections, support, or solutions. The focus stays only on one person's problems, which can be limiting and even harmful depending on the topic. This awareness can help you understand the need to balance venting with more constructive conversations.

This highlights the need for a change in how we approach venting conversations. If you or someone you talk to often engages in venting, recognize the strain it can put on both the speaker and listener. Venting should be used sparingly as a resource, not the go-to solution for every conversation.

Another key point about venting conversations is understanding that they often provide only temporary relief.

After venting, you might feel a bit better because it frees up mental and emotional space, letting you focus on other parts of your life. A good venting session can help you get back on track by clearing your mind. While these moments can show the benefits of venting, it's important to remember that these benefits don't last long.

With the insights gained from this section, it's important to know how to use venting conversations effectively. While venting can be a helpful way to relieve stress, it's essential not to depend only on it. After you've had a chance to vent, think about what else you need to do to fully address your concerns. Look for solutions that help you move beyond just venting and open up to more positive and joyful conversations. This approach creates a healthier balance and leads to more fulfilling interactions.

Creating buy-in

Some conversations aim to get others to agree with your point of view. This might be on purpose, but often, you might not realize your conversation is going in this direction. As we explore this topic, try to stay open-minded, even if it feels a bit uncomfortable. The goal is to understand your conversations better and make any necessary changes to improve your future interactions.

Let's discuss buy-in conversations. These are conversations where you share your thoughts and perspectives on a topic. You often highlight all the relevant points that support your viewpoint. In these discussions, it's clear where you stand and why you think the way you do.

Understanding the value of buy-in conversations is important. These talks are valuable because they boost your confidence in your opinion. They help you explain why you think a certain way and convince others to see your point of view. This can be very helpful and sometimes, it's exactly the kind of conversation you need to have.

However, these conversations can become less helpful when they turn into repetitive micro conversations and other perspectives are needed. It's important to notice when a conversation is stuck in a cycle and to be open to new viewpoints. This can prevent the conversation from becoming unproductive and make it more beneficial.

Sometimes, our points of view are seasonal. You might adopt a particular stance to get through a tough time. But what happens when that period is over? What do you do when it's time to move on to something new, and your old way of thinking no longer works? This is where buy-in conversations can become challenging.

Let's explore another aspect of buy-in conversations. We've already talked about how you present your information. Now, let's see how these conversations can involve trying to convince others to agree with you and ignoring other viewpoints. In a buy-in conversation, you might strongly believe that your perspective is the only right one.

When considering if you're having buy-in conversations, think about it on a topic-by-topic basis. Some topics might naturally have a stricter tone, like religious beliefs or family standards. However, other topics, like your views on work situations or your approach to dating, might not need to be as fixed.

Understanding the context of each topic helps you determine if your conversation style is appropriate or if it needs to be more flexible.

When thinking about changing buy-in conversations because of their impact, ask yourself if this type of conversation is really meeting your needs. Are you getting what you need from these discussions? Consider if you need to keep this tone with some people and not others. Being aware of this creates accountability for how you handle the information you have.

Does it have purpose?

Let's revisit why it's important to talk about these things in the first place. Your conversations create space for certain topics in your everyday life. This book is about helping you change and grow. It's not about evaluating every conversation all the time—that would be exhausting. Instead, it's about being mindful of how your conversations can influence how you live your life.

When you're thinking about whether or not to talk about something, keep a few things in mind. Consider how you'll feel and what you'll think after having these conversations. Are they helping you move in the direction you want to go? Are they supporting your goals and well-being? By reflecting on these points, you can make more thoughtful decisions about your conversations.

If your conversations aren't helping you move forward, make a change. If they don't have any impact, it's okay to leave them as they are. But if they don't represent you well, it's time to adjust. If you find that a conversation style is working for you, keep it. Just remember to check in with yourself from time to time to make sure everything is still aligned with your goals and well-being.

Chapter Nine

Ensuring Long-Term Communication Success

Your micro conversations are a valuable resource for your growth. These internal and external dialogues help you make decisions and take action. For example, when you see something interesting in a sales ad, you start imagining how it would look in your home. This mental picture sparks a micro conversation about the experiences you'll have with that item. In those brief moments, you decide to purchase it. Depending on when you actually buy it, you might continue these internal conversations or start talking about it with others.

The key to harnessing the power of micro conversations lies in being more intentional about what you focus on during these dialogues. By doing so, you can better direct your thoughts and actions towards your goals and growth.

Creating the shift in your conversations

Changing long-standing habits can require more effort than you might expect. It's easy to stick with routines because they become effortless over time, designed to remove the need for constant decision-making. These routines can be beneficial and be exactly what you need during certain periods. However, when these habits no longer yield the desired results, it's time to change. Recognizing this need for change is the first step towards creating new, more effective routines.

The first thing I will discuss for making this change is a layered approach. A layered approach means not expecting yourself to completely overhaul how you talk about things all at once. Instead, you can choose one part of how you discuss a topic, focus on mastering that change, and then move on to the next part. This way, you gradually build new habits and make sustainable changes.

Before I give some examples of what this looks like. I want to talk about why it is important. Sometimes you do things that don't feel authentic to who you are. Your history becomes the identifier that this is just who I am and how I do things. There is truth to that. It's in the history. The reality is in while this is how you have done things, it's not in line with what you want. Your value of change is in your results. You have to learn to become the person who is in line with the results that you want to have. I think that is worth repeating.

"You have to learn to become the person who is in line with the results that you want to have."

And therefore the layered approach is a style that I recommend to changing your conversations. You want to master the steps and make them your own. When you do this, you give yourself time to identify yourself with the new style.

So, what does taking a layered approach look like?

One way of doing this is mapping your conversations presently. In this book, we have talked about themes to the conversations, how you present information, and what kinds of topics you discuss. These are just a few things that make up your conversation. The idea is behind breaking down the relevant parts about how you are having these conversations and then finding one part to focus on changing.

Let's say you want to work on changing the topics of your discussions. You find you spend most of your time talking about problems in your relationship. It requires no effort to complain about something your partner has done. The layer to this conversation is to find one trait about your partner that you value or see potential in for growth. Once you identify how can you present this topic from a genuine place, then you might move in to actually having this conversation with someone else, which means intentionally knowing who would be the best person to have this new conversation with.

That first layer of the topic is going to require some effort to find. While you are finding the new topic, you are most likely going to still be engaged in conversations that are the problems of your partner. Hopefully, with some greater awareness of the need for change, but the energy to change it isn't happening yet. You are building the area of just finding the new topics first before putting them into action. The better you get at finding the new topics, your mastery can go in to how you are referring to them. As you feel validated by the conversation you experience in focusing on a new topic and how you describe it. There is a comfort in putting it out there for someone else's feedback.

Each layer is about growing in your strength and abilities to see the new approach. To get familiar with it.

Checks and balances

When something is on your mind, it feels important to talk about. If I'm thinking about it, it must need my attention. If I'm considering it, then others should know, right?

I am here to say not always. Sometimes the conversation is one you have already had one too many times. You have it enough times that the person you are talking to, even yourself, can replay what you are going to say before you say it.

What it means if it is on your mind is that it has significance in some way to you. Or you are in ongoing environments that influence you to think about it. It does not mean that you need to give conversation to it.

So how do you change up something that continually comes up but isn't something that you need to give space to in your life? This is checks and balances. You are going to start with the check portion of this.

The checks are check-ins with yourself on the topic being influenced for you to consider. You are going to ask yourself a few questions.

Why is this coming up for me?

- Is talking about something with someone important to getting the results I am looking for? (Results being validation, acknowledgement, problem solving, etc.)

- Is this something that I need to give time to reflect on? Is it time for me to change how I reflect on it?

These are just some examples of check-in questions you can ask yourself. There are also times that you can use the check-in questions with trusted people in your life for accountability. The point of the check-in is to determine whether the conversation is something that is relevant to have. If it is, whether the way you are initially wanting to have it is the most effective. You will want to have a conversation, but you have had it so many times before, that it becomes a roadblock or a distraction more than a resource.

Take the time necessary to check in, to determine the value of the conversation, before giving time to it. You also might find that this process is just what you need to address it.

So, what are the balances of "checks and balances?" It is where you consider if there is a balance in perspective around a topic. Conversations can take a primary perspective on how you have them. You can talk about work and it primarily focuses on what you don't like about work. In this focus, it would be seen as you don't like what you do and maybe it is time for a change. Alternate perspectives to the conversation would be to balance it with what you do like, or maybe it is to consider ways you would change what you don't like.

To balance out the conversation for yourself and others, consider whether you always approach a topic from just one point of view. Reflect on how you discuss the topic and ask yourself if you're presenting it in the same way every time. Are you focusing on the positives or negatives only? By recognizing this pattern, you can adjust your perspective.

Think about your relationship with your child. You often find yourself fixated on what your child isn't accomplishing, which leads to conversations centered on your frustrations as a parent. This pattern can feel repetitive, like a song stuck on repeat. To balance these conversations, try focusing on your child's strengths and how they can apply those strengths to make better choices. Alternatively, start problem-solving to understand why these issues persist. By balancing the conversation, you allow yourself to experience this topic from a different, more constructive perspective.

Implementing a simple checks-and-balances process for changing your conversations can create a level of accountability. This process helps you understand how what you are saying influences you. It involves regularly reviewing the topics you discuss and the way you approach them.

Check-ins

Check-ins are different from what we discussed in checks and balances. This version of check-ins is not about the topic of discussion. It has to do with where you are mentally or emotionally before you have a conversation.

Part of why you are learning about micro conversations is centered on what we are talking about right now. Conversations are influencing your mind about what you are thinking. Your interpretation of both present and future situations. You may enter a conversation with one perspective and come out on the other side with a shift in perspective. Understanding this is what can empower you to align your conversations to be supportive of the direction you are looking to go on a topic.

Conversations also have the ability to shift your emotions and your mood. Think about some conversations you have had. Have any of them left you feeling excited, motivated, or inspired? That on completing that conversation, you get into motion on the task at hand.

There are also those conversations where you are done with them feeling drained, frustrated, or irritated. When done with the conversations, you just want to be left alone. Maybe you no longer want to be a part of the experience you originally were so motivated to do.

Considering for yourself what conversations influence you in one direction or another gives you a set of information for change. This is where your check-ins come into place. That space of awareness prior to conversation. Being able to ask yourself what is going on for me before the conversations.

That initial check-in can also aid in determining if a conversation should be had. It can help you know who you want to have this conversation with. It is your degree of intentionality that says I want to make sure this conversation results in an experience that is conducive to what I need.

Your follow-up check-in is your space to determine if this conversation provided you what you need. Was it the type of conversation that influenced you in the direction that you needed to go on the topic? Did it help you shift your feelings on the topic, looking at the conversation to see how it fits into your overall experience?

You hold yourself accountable for getting what you need from micro conversations by checking in with yourself.

Deciding when it is time to change your conversations

Remember, it is not about evaluating every conversation you have. There are conversations you have that will have parts to them that don't align with a goal. Or you will find yourself in favor of one perspective at one time and another one at a different time.

There are some key things that will help you decide if there are conversations that need to shift in order to make changes.

For a moment, I want you to consider if there is anything in your life you are working on as a goal. Big or small. Maybe you are trying to get more organized. You have tried multiple systems to help you achieve this goal. Unfortunately, you are cycling in and out of success. You might question yourself on whether this is a goal you will ever achieve. It takes on a toll of hopelessness. With others, they might have comments like, "You have never been organized; it's just not your thing." Or maybe you are saying to yourself, "This is pointless. I spend more energy trying to change versus just dealing with the ways things are."

This example describes a situation where your conversation about the desired change is not supporting the direction you want to go. The direction of these conversations supports you giving up on the task and continue to identify yourself as an unorganized person.

When this goal has value to you, it is not only important to work on the skills of being organized but also your conversation around it. This is when you want to get more intentional about your conversations.

You want the conversations to be like, "I am working one step at a time to get organized. At some point, I will find the right system for me." This provides a place of hope, accountability, and time to become more organized. Your response to this type of conversation continues to support the direction of you becoming more organized.

Another indicator of when you want to work on your conversation has to do with the conversation with other people.

Take, for instance, you have seen some struggles with your partner in your relationship. You can't seem to see eye to eye on something like parenting. You have your way you feel is right and they have theirs. In the conversations you are having with your partner, your explanation will continually point out why they need to do things your way. Saying something like, "I have used this with her and she does better with this approach. Your way is not helping." Or maybe you would say something like, "That is the way you were raised, but I don't want my children to be raised like that."

In conversations that continually have the same points made, the person you are talking to will most likely be able to say what you are going to say before you say it. Or they will respond in a way that addresses what they believe you are going to say. This conversation reflects a place where there is value to change. Repeating the same conversations makes people lose interest because they already assume what you're going to say.

Taking the time to shift these kinds of conversations supports making sure one another stays present. It also supports your accountability to not be redundant in conversations. It's easy to get off-topic in these conversations and not talk about what's relevant today. Or not being present to what can change in you or them as it relates to a topic in the present?

If your conversations with others have become predictable then it is most likely time to review whether the conversation is supportive of what you are looking to create.

An additional sign that it is time to change your conversation has to do with your personal experience with it. If you find yourself shifted in a way that you don't value the conversation. Then why keep having it?

This is not about giving up on what the conversation might be about. It is about understanding that it is not serving you in a way that you want to show up and have it.

If you are having a conversation about workload. You continually are addressing the countless number of things you need to get done. Your focus is on the inability to keep up, the lack of consideration your boss has to what you need, or how it conflicts with what else you want to be doing with your time.

Whether this conversation is being had internally or with someone else, your experience at the moment the topic is presented is to check out so you don't have to be bothered.

That's when you know it is time. To let go of this style of talking about things.

Avoiding the conversation is not always the method of change.

In this example, there may be value in you addressing the imbalance in your workload and expectations of your boss.

The sign for change is about the need to have a different way you go about it, both for you to be better grounded in your experience as well as for you to work towards the change you are looking to accomplish.

Exposure is the name of the game

Your conversations are a part of what creates an experience for you. In your conversations, you continually shape what something looks like. You ever had those moments when you are talking with someone about an event you both were at? Only to find that the way you remember it is different from their experience.

Your conversation around a topic is the way you describe and remember the details. It is what you are buying into. This is also what you continue to make future decisions from. You want to make sure your conversations are in line with the type of experience that supports who you are and what you want to have in your life.

If something is going to keep showing up in your life, wouldn't it be important to ensure its something you truly want?

Lots of things are happening in your life from one day to the next. Not everything in your encounters has the same value for what you need to maintain experience around. Taking the intentional look at whether you give space for it in your conversations is to decide if that experience is allowed to continue to grow in your world.

It is also important to remember that your conversations are about what is influencing your abilities to make changes. Throughout, we have talked about how both internal and external conversations show up to influence our thoughts, feelings, and actions. When you are looking to make significant changes in your life. Part of your change is what you are saying.

You want to expose yourself to conversations that are going to challenge in the direction you want to go. Provide correction that is healthy and helpful. To stop conversations that contradict the goal you are looking to achieve. Your conversational experiences are all about the space where you are doing life. You want to make sure that you are intentionally creating that space.

Your conversations matter

In becoming more intentional about your micro conversations, I want you to value three things to support your why. First, your time matters. A lot of time is given to the conversations you are having within yourself. Thinking about the things of the past, considering the possibilities of the future, or reflecting on present-day options. If you are given time to think about it, wouldn't it make sense for it to be a resource to you, not a roadblock?

Second, you want to guide conversations to have influence over you. Whether you want to manage your mood and emotions better so that your days are in a better state of being or maybe you are trying to make some life changes, the perspective you take in your conversations on a topic makes a difference. When it is necessary, be mindful of your conversation's influence over your change.

Lastly, if you are going to speak about something. Make sure your voice counts for the things you want to represent. Your conversation is one representative way in how you show up in your life. People's experiences of you are partly influenced by how you have conversations. It can determine others' level of engagement with you. It can support what others feel safe in talking with you about. Your conversations are a supportive part of how you let others know what you are about. Make it count for what works for you.

Review

Thank you for your time!

Here is a quick link to review on Amazon. If you purchased through another outlet would love for you to review there as well. Thank you